DEST☉RYER ☉F EMPIRE

DESTORYER OF EMPIRE

COLLECTED POEMS: 2020 - 2022

Natureza Gabriel

COLLECTED POEMS

EMPIRE OF BEAUTY

The Nike of Samothrace	1
The Many Good Uses of Apocalyse	6
7th Planetary Boundary Breached	14
A General Astride his Horse	19
3:29 AM	27
Six Years	36
On the Seventh Day, Rest	63
Requiem for an empire	79

DOMES OF LIGHT

For Pete Jackson, March 16	85
Look How Amazing	88
Life Is Beautiful	93
A Proper Accounting	98
The Dome of Light	104
Kalpa	110
Murmurs	120
Spatial Geometries of the Human Form	129
Domes of Light	133

APPRENTICE TO GRIEF

Apprentice to grief	141
Descent	159

DESTORYER OF EMPIRE

I Don't Need a License	169
The Vassals of rome	174
Dawn on the Last Day of the First Day	191

EMPIRE OF BEAUTY

(2021)

Perseus of Macedon was a Basileus (Emperor) of Macedon at the time of the Third Macedonian War, in 168 BC, when the Roman Empire conquered Macedonia. Leader of an earth-based peole, he was subjugated by the Romans, imprisoned in a dungeon, and killed by depriving him of sleep. This poem cycle, a meditation on the birth and death of empires, toggles between the perspective of Perseus, at various times in his life, and the author, writing in America in 2022, as eco-systems fail, and the echo of the Roman Empire embodied in the United States of America teeters on the verge of collapse.

I

THE NIKE OF SAMOTHRACE

I exist where the wave meets the Ocean.
Where deepest yearning meets identity.
Where everything you've ever been in this Life
And all the songlines you've tread before,
Unite in the feeling of this present moment.

It is 4 am and rain beats down on the roof.
Somewhere a cat sleeps, sphinx-like.
The conquerors, when they came, cut off the heads and noses of the great statues
Because those who made them were animists,
And knew the God could come into the stone.
Those who built this world began by beheading the last.
They cut the nose off the Sphinx so she could not breathe.
Deprived of breath, the God withers they believed.

But is it so?
And who is deprived of breath?
COVID comes, taking our breath.
A knee on the neck of George Floyd-
Taking the breath.
Chainsaws in the Amazon, taking the breath.
The conquerors of this modern world

came, extinguishing the breath-
But of whom?

I contemplate the Nike of Samothrace,
Winged Victory,
Headless in the Louvre.
Plundered by a Frenchman from a rubble pile in the Aegean.
Placed on a pedestal,
Fetishized like an animal taxidermied in a zoo.
The statue has no head.

And yet Winged Victory does.
Painstakingly,
And painfully as well,
I grow her a new head, in my mind's eye.
And yet, through the transmutation of Unity
Find that it is, in fact, myself who is growing a new head.

All heads are born from hearts
This is the neuro-embryonic way.
A drumbeat in your ears lays down neural wiring
Firing
In Cascades
Lacelines of meaning
Sonic signatures of rememberance.

Remembrance.
That was dis-membered

By history
By greed
By war
Conquest
Power over.

Singing sung lucid dreamed
Back into vividness.

From the stump of a neck
Veins, sinew, animated by Spirit
By requirement to know itself,
Re-assembling
Like councils long disbanded
Re-aligning
Like songlines paved over
Re-constituting
Like alliances governed
By a shared vision of peace.

From my heart flows upward
My head coming together.
Deep within its center the memories
Of everything that ever was.

A listening that drops to the furnace
At the center of the Earth &
Rises to the shaking of the Stars

It is all alive

Humming with mystery

Vision opening
The ability to see,
The ability to see through
Piercing
Penetrating
The veils that would obscure us from what
    simply is.

A wreath around her head,
For she was wearing one
Isn't simply a wreath.

These leaves twisted by Divine hands
Into a crown, an amulet, a bower are in fact
Her antennae.

Sensory apparatuses–
Conveying the living pattern intelligence.
Clairvoyance.
Clairaudience.
Clairsentience.
Synaesthesia.

How words fall short, all of them.

I bow to the Nike of Somathrace,
Winged Victory.
Beheaded by Rome,

Which fell once
And whose imprint is falling again.

Arises here, now,
The opportunity to find the place
In the center of the center of the center
Where the wave meets the Ocean–

For that is who we are.

2

THE MANY GOOD
USES OF APOCALYPSE

For two thousand years your progenitors have
 been mating with something dead.
Vampires and necrophiliacs, these are your
 grandfathers white boy.
I too came to a party thrown I thought for me–
Baccanalian, orgiastic, Playboy bunnies, cocaine,
 people lighting cigars with hundred dollar
 bills.

Curious to see the Pax Romano with our own
 eyes
We came forward in a phalanx to see the
 Romans, legion
Arrayed as far as eye could see, a number of them
 seated on the backs of Elephants.

The year was a 168 BC, the place an island in the
 Aegean,
What you know now as the third Macedonian
 War.

Empires come and go, topple over one another
 but
When they cut the heads off of the gods at

Samothrace to kill them
Sliced the nose off the Sphinx to deprive her of breath
There was a genocidal glee in all this destruction that surpassed
In its systematization what you had imagined.

Have you seen the humans, lately?
My mentor, a legend, tells me of a dream he tracked,
Falling from the sky, a sky altar dropping him down,
Conscious, to the earth plane, beside him, fully awake
A woman falling too, and he seeing her, a twin meteor,
Plummeting to Earth.

On impact he hits the ground, fearful of the pain in his knees
Sprints to the opening of a cave nearby, hunkers down against the wall.
She, walking in, looks around, asks him–
Why are you hiding?
Him–*Have you seen them, the humans?*

A crude lot.
This is what happens when you fuck something dead generation upon generation
Hoard up dead dollars sucked from living souls,

Crushed from your brothers and sisters
Kill off all the witches
Turn the trees into board feet
The earth's veins into rings for your fingers.
If you fuck death for long enough, something unwell starts to happen to your brain.

The pandemic lets up for two seconds
We hop back on aeroplanes, cross the ocean, burn carbon
Like a smoker who'd been forced to cut a three pack-a-day habit overnight
Suddenly unleashed in a gas station convenience store
Where behind the cashier's head are arrayed cartons over cartons
Of cigarettes in the bleachwash of fluorescent lights.
Praise God, I can become a chimney again, we think.
It is like this.

Smokestacks of the lungs, ferry me away from all this loss.
Inhale, meditative deep.
Carry me away from all this suffering we have unleashed upon ourselves.
The nicotine hits us, we hold it deep in the lungs/
It washes over

And the pain dulls.

But the cure for the pain is in the pain, says
    Roberto.

Unleash us back into the world
unrestrain us so that we may burn
Carbon
At the top of the teepee is the opening where
    smoke rises.
Close the flap, it festers accumulating.
Tie down the edges of the cloth to the ground
    and there you have us,
Our world in micro-cosm.
The atmosphere a teepee, us the fire tenders.
You'd think we'd try to put out the fire but *No*.

Forty generations of death fuckers, and instead
    we are throwing
Logs on that bitch like there's no tomorrow.
Let's burn the house down around us with us in it.
And while this, did you notice there is 30% off
    on last season's denim?
    What an adjectival deal.

We think the death is in the pandemic, over
    there.
But the death is in us– we've been face-fucking it
    for millennia.
The pandemic only moving over us, slowly,

An Angel of Death, a gentle magnet,
Pulling on the latent metals in our body.
Magnetizing what is just beneath the surface,
    trying to get out.

No one has the right to life.
No one has the right even to the body they're
    wearing.
All of this on loan from a beneficent Universe
From our Holy Mother, from the Earth herself.

Not one atom that comprises the aggregate
    assemblage
We know as ourselves belongs in actuality to us.

We are weightless breath.
We are the dream of a unified field.
All the matter in the world was made by other
    than us.
Belongs to the Creator.
We are renters only,
Strutting around like we own the joint.

But we like the shape death gives us.
Suburbia and rivers of oil to drive upon.
We worship at the great altar of the Profit & the
    Loss.

Our Mother, the Earth, she misses us
But imagine for a moment that if in Harry Potter

We might not find ourselves working for the side
   we thought we were.

What if, instead of our mother eating all the
   carbon we burn
We had to consume it ourselves?
What if that tailpipe was the inlet to your lungs
That lack of respect
Lack of appreciation
We pay to the Mother were our true bank
   account,
Not some pileage of coin.

What if our retirement accounts were
   relationships?

It is/
they are.

In Spirit we are poor or rich also.
To decolonize the mind, perhaps, is to extract
   yourself
From Death worship, death fuckery,
All death ways.

Harder than we realize.
Twenty one hundred years later I returned, to be
   educated by Rome,
So I could understand Empire.
Came back to destroy her this time,

Then realized I don't have to.

She is destroying herself.
Let the dead bury their dead.

Rather then, I will de-story her by putting a full shoulder
Behind another dream.

A dream of the unified field.
A Lifeway.
An unlearning.
A re-birth, not a stillbirth.

Sing in me muse,
Dreaming at the edge of collapse.

My friend Will, one day
Decades ago, engaged in missionary medical work
Traveling in the highlands of Guatemala encountered a mother
Who said, *There's a monster inside my boy.*
Said Will and fellow doctors, *How do you mean?*
Watch this, said she, holding a piece of bacon above the boy's open mouth, age ten.
Boy tilts back his head, opens wide.
Snaking up the throat comes the worm to grab the bacon from the woman's outstretched hand.

Pickled in formaldehyde later, the monster who
   turned out many meters long, was removed
   from the boy,
But we moderns, all of us, have that thing inside.
That is the death wish, the inner apocalypse,
   latent.

Find yours quick and get it out,
Else when the great storms come,
It will become enchanted by them and fuse.
Then the death seeking within and the death
   seeking without will grant the latent
Wish, and you won't be here with us anymore.

3

7TH PLANETARY
B⊕UNDARY BREACHED

7th planetary boundary breached
And poems flow out of me like bleeding.

I can barely speak in ordinary language.
I rise, and run, not walk to the Land,
Press my hands into service, making the
    beautiful.

Hold tight your loved ones
Bring them close...
Yet I say now is the time to build
An empire of beauty

What are the technical parameters of an empire
    of beauty?
And what makes it an empire anyway?
I have deep aversion to that word.

The Empire extant in my neck of the woods
Worships at the altar of the profit and the loss.
Everyone wants a piece of the American pie
But we have forgotten who owns the bakery, says
    Tiokasin.

In truth, we own nothing.
The scaffolds that run the rhythms of our bodies
 are celestial.
The meat of us itself on loan from the universe.
Even our food we do not digest: it is other
 creatures living inside us makes most of that
 happen.

Down here, it's all *ubuntu*.
I am because we are.

Contracted isolated selves, not knowing the
 greater body
Thinking thought lines alienated from the
 Original Instructions
Is the origin of this particular catastrophic frame.

The Greater I, in the form of a Bezos, a Musk, a
 Branson, built a spaceship
An aspirational model of my own erect cock
Blasted it into the atmosphere
But billions and billions of dollars later
Noted that when the adrenaline wore off
I was nowhere

All the beauty
Receded away from me as I left our mother.
Like a jeweled marble in a vastness of vantablack,
Even leaving at velocity she was the only thing
 that looked like home.

So in reality,
What we must do,
If it all comes apart at the seams
Is quietly gather at a spot in the woods
Decided upon in advance

near a placed Robert Frost pointed out years ago
A fork in the road, two small paths.
You'll know it because one is less traveled by

Down that road
And that road only
Which will be dirt
Not paved at all

You will find us sitting in a circle
Around a fire
Telling once again the old stories,
Tending the babies
Caring for the Elders
Who are carrying wisdom

Tracking our dreams/
Weaving a culture.

Because the Empire of Beauty,
The Ladder of Nature
Is already here to mimic.
Is waiting for us to ascend.

Its sovereigns our actual Mother, our Actual
    Father.
The celestial court known to all of us in our birth
    charts.

I look to you now, Mother and Father,
Through the implements I carry
I hold you in my hands.

Tell us, Mother Moon
Tell us, Father Sun

In what way shall we teach the story
Of your greater glory
Of the way you hold it all together
Teaching us how to live

The proper posture
In relation to all this beauty
Is kneeling
Close the Earth

Who is alive.

Our prayer must become
stronger and stronger
Until it compels us into action
Shakes us from the narcissistic haze.

The time is now.

Awaken all ye
Listeners

Hear the great drum
Beating in your ears.

Life calls itself to Order.
Summons us to the great task at hand.

Cortisol in a crescendo
Is the pre-requisite for the foetal ejection reflex

Now is the time to find
What love came here to do — right Skeena?

It's not a push
It's an innate slingshot
Ejection reflex

It is the way something living is born
At the exact moment it needs to be.

4

A GENERAL ASTRIDE HIS H⊕RSE

A General astride his horse galloping toward me
As I, one Perseus, Basileus of Macedon,
Do by just decree

Implore you fellows loyal to our ancient way
Delay not in heeding the warnings of this
    Council /

My father fought them twice
When I was but a boy
And came home battle-weary not only
But spirit-weary,
His soul itself heavy /

And went and settled himself in the great baths
Muttering.
I peaked round the corner of a column to espy
    him seated
Chest deep in steaming water
His face buried in his hands – I grew afraid

Departed he then, for the Temple of the Greater
    Gods
To seek counsel and consolation
I had not before seen him wrought up in this way.

A year later perhaps
One day out hunting with him
We paused on a hillside overlook/

Me eating a fistful of berries fresh gathered
He set his hand upon my shoulder and said
    nothing less than
I have seen the end of the world

I shuddered, turned toward him without
    removing his arm
Which lay upon me now like deadweight.
Twice I have fought them, he continued.
*But I am not convinced any longer that they are
    human.*

I would need to lose a battle
Flee
Becoming imprisoned
Paraded through the streets of Rome manacled
On a Festive Day
Be spat upon by ladies in finery eating apples
And skewered meats
Kept in the dark in a dungeon at Alba Fucens
Underground
Forty days deprived of sleep until slipping in
    delirium
Across the threshold into death

Come back in a body
Twenty centuries later
Be educated in the armpit of the echo of their
    Empire
To understand his words.

I am not convinced any longer that they are
    human.

It is a dangerous thing to declare one less than or
    more than anything

The moderns (as an aside) have misconstrued
    our conception of the flatness of the world

It was not so much a geometric as a political
    observation

Down here, we are all midwifed by soil
Stand between 10 and 15 hands tall.
We are the same height
Like a field of grass growing under the same
    summer sun.

To say that someone is more than or less than
Plants the psychic seeds of aggrandizement or
    diminishment
Neither of which bear good fruit.

Yet now I understand what he meant /

And for a moment I miss my father

Obsessed with tabulation,
The Romans built an Empire leaning on one half
    of their minds.

I stand accused by history
Of not marshaling all of my resources
In the battle of Pydna
In the Third Macedonian War

The Romans brought elephants
Our warriors fought in a phalanx
There was a break in the terrain

Why didn't I call the cavalry?
Et cetera Et cetera

History says I held something back
I don't deny it

What I held back
However what not merely or even principally
    troops

I held back beauty

I didn't pour into it
Everything of Spirit that could have been poured
    in

Something stilled my hand

/

I should explain what a Basileus is:

There are two words that get translated into proto-Greek
Meaning chieftain
But then as empire waxes gather connotation of Emperor

One is Archon, the other Basileus
Feel even in your mouth the difference between these
As it holds worlds.

Archon the same root as architecture
Authority conveyed by structure

Basileus, friend, it means the Living Law.

What is then, the Living Law?

Inhale deeply.

To explain this I will need to originate your Mind elsewhere.

Once upon a time the words were animals.

Not like, or as– there was no metaphor, no simile.

There were then word-priests
Who spoke the Sacred into Being.
It, numinous, was already there.
We, simply, spoke it into human speech.

It could not but be Spoken
In alignment with Original Instructions

Because what was not thus made
Could not be voiced.

This language only operated as a conduit
Bringing into word-form the thought-forms of Nature.

My role: bridge
The Living World, the World of Man.
My charge and obligation: Harmony.

Came then upon me an Empire
The Romans, as they came to be known
And I perceived them speaking a tongue–

How can I say it?

–That was dead.

Some things change a little
Some things change a lot
The year is 2022.
Rome has succeeded in sucking all into its belly–
Digesting the world, which was its aim

Somehow,
Beautiful Jesus was co-opted by them as well
Became a propagation vector.

The church of Rome–
Erected around the most humble Nazarene–
declares Terra Nullius /
Declares the Living Law a void
Grants itself authority to step in and take.

Here we are
Twenty two hundred years later
At the closing, not the opening curtain
And I have returned.

All the ornaments of Rome are here,
Zuckerberg quoting passages of the Aeneid, can't
    you see?

In a broad ellipse
I come back to carry forward
What I set down 2200 years ago

To put the head back on the Nike

Re-unite the sentient fabric of the Living Law
With fellow sovereigns of like heart and mind

As Rome immolates itself
Another dead thing collapsing under the weight
 of its emptiness,
Trying to bring all Life down with it,
Which it won't.

I bow to what is Dead
Because understanding that is necessary to teach
 us
What is truly Alive.

5

3.29 AM

I rise at 3.29 AM
Know it because I check the clock
Lie back down
Listen to the blood beating in my ears
Hear cadences of rhythm sluicing through my mind

A poem a filter
To sieve the grief into beauty

I remember
Lines of verse that came to me/
Through me/
Twenty-five years ago
That I didn't understand at the time

Fragments arriving
With syllabic architecture
Ornament and vividness
But uncohered yet
Masses in primordial soup
Not yet condensed into story

Recall a cross-country drive
Was I nineteen?

From New Haven to St. Louis/
Pulling off in a woodland feathered with fern
Somewhere in Pennsylvania
To scribble down a poem
Uncoiling down out of my mind a long snake
A fragment of DNA
Transcribing itself

Recall the shock
Of reading Jorie Graham's *The Dream of A
    Unified Field*:
An illuminated manuscript
Poems humming themselves
Into completely lucid apparitions
Substantive enough to walk into
Vivid enough to awaken paintings in my mind
A physics of becoming/
The truest science I've read

Found myself in Iowa City in these years
About a girl
Walked into the writing department at this
    university
That wasn't mine

Foundnd Jorie's mailbox
And left in it
A small poem
Some words I don't even remember what
Unable to resist a call and response

I needed to tell her that her words awakened
Worlds in me
Surfaced something ancient
I could not yet name

Pierced the veil
United art and science

It worked, I want to yell
Embracing her–
Not Jorie–
But the Muse itself
You did it
You dreamed the field united
I felt it in my chest
My eyes welled up with tears knowing its truth

A conundrum
Rightly wrangled
A moral dilemma
studied in the body
And suddenly a trapdoor opens deep in the palm
    of my hand
The feeling inward electric/

A void / a space
In the arm where there wasn't one

A tunnel running all the way into my heart

A somatic experience/
Pins and needles
Some awakening

I shut down thinking
Choke it off through meditative effort
This is why I've practiced all these years/
So I could simply turn it off
And drop into the infinity of sensation

A world opens
Humming discourse
In spatial geometries of the human form
An archeology of shadows
The space within electric
Some vast equation seeking to understand itself

Who am I?

Beneath thinking, effort, morality, conception

The car I bought in October
I named Sky Chariot
Before I remembered this previous incarnation

We come again and again
Doused through the Veil of Forgetting so we
    don't trip over the traumas of our past lives

But these imprints hover
At the edge of consciousness
Flicker and beckon at the edge of sleep
Unbidden, the mind flicking out
Patterns traceries arabesques
A moment of remembrance disguised as dream or fancy

What use, memory
If we can't harvest all of ourselves?

A practice a filter we feed ourselves through
To catch a glimpse
Of our yearning
Our tenderness
The shape of our particular love
Our particular gift

Painting on canvas
Sculpting in stone
Or these words here

We use Art to throw ourselves against the world
Toss our particular grain of sand into the Ocean
Let her take us/ break us
Throw us around/
Wash us ashore

Maybe we'll catch a glimpse of who we really are

⊕ ⊕ ⊕

I do not believe in my heart of hearts that the
    world is ending
It cannot end anymore than it can begin

Yet does so each day for those dying and those
    being born
As someone much wiser than I explained

But we could end
Humanity as known to itself

As known through this civilization so-called
Could end
This empire.

Idled in a mall parking lot
Now it's 4.31 AM I see by the clock on the dash
I've come to feed my horses
in the form of an electric car
My chariot this lifetime eats electrons
It's belly is lithium-ion
Only I've managed to forget my wallet

So here I sit, looking out across acres of asphalt
Punctuated by sodium lights
Ringed by the haloes of storefronts
Their signage neon illumined.

It is so devoid of beauty, this.
My town in America
Has no city centre
Has no commons
No acropolis
Only this

It is not dirty
But its deadness is at no time more apparent
    than 4 am.

How are we to commune at the marketplace?
To vivify our souls?

It would be as if the ancient cities were excavated
And there were no temple sites
No squares
No plazas
But only stalls and stalls of vendors
The ruins of houses and ancient parking lots
Houses and ancient parking lots

How devoid of beauty

My job/ duty/ obligation
Is to string together transparent lacelines of
    meaning

Weave new fabrics
Open possible doors

I've known this for some time
Even before I'd suffered enough

At the origin of consciousness a crime scene
A devastation that shakes us awake
Slaps us from the trance of an inherited world

Trauma thus the gateway to our own becoming.
It's healing the reclamation of our purpose.

Don't be fooled:
The wound generates the medicine required to
   heal it
IF

A thousand shards of distraction are avoided
You don't sink into drink
Or victimization
Or bitterness
Or blame

We are cut open/
Flayed out wide

And either the wound festers
Grows gangrenous
Kills us slowly or quick

OR ELSE
We turn toward it
Abandon hope and enter deep in study
Of its particular gift
Until it transforms us/
And we return from the Other shore
Healed
And with medicine for our people.

I teach three things that are one thing:
Healing, Sovereignty, and what is required to
    inherit our possible beauty

SIX YEARS

I commend myself to your Generals
Colonel Sanders and his ilk

All brave soldiers
Who hawk militant chicken
And kneel on necks, etc etc

The army expends billions and billions
Of dead coin on research projects
Training Artificial Intelligence
To pilot warplanes

We perfect the Art of Death
While all around us eco-systems collapse
Homeless wander through downtown
San Francisco defecating
Outdoors/
Tripping over Brothers and Sisters
Passed out in an alleyway
Syringe still stuck in the arm

Flattened by concentrated Opiates
Dreams required to escape
This hellhole madness

My transit to the other side
The far bank of this river
Was not graceful.

I didn't climb into an *ikyak*
Or *oolokton*,
There was no anthropometric kayak
There for me.

I stumbled screaming into floodwaters
My backside burning
Dove into the breach to douse the flames
Was carried then
By currents stronger that myself

Nothing elegant about it

That I reached the further shore
A Miracle

People say–
I cannot stomach all this madness
This civilization so-called
Abducts me from myself
But when I stand in what makes sense
To my heart
I feel crazy.

Brother–
Let me tell you something about crazy/

Because assuredly I can name that tune.

I've been through the backside of crazy
Shat backwards out the devil's arsehole

Held together by the only thing stronger
Than entropy,
That being love.

That being the absolute refusal
Of the weave of the Universe to collapse
Despite the fragility of our Psyches
Which can indeed do so

That being the absolute refusal
Of my Wife, my Dad, my friend Mitchel
To let me go/
Until I was just pinioned there on the rock
Alone with my alienation

Seeing the Sun
Hit the carapace of my body
Not feeling the Light at all.

My bitter refusal to allow
Events of the past to be fully real

Can we stand in our hearts
Without dissociating
And make a big enough circle to hold

All the tragedy
Without leaving ourselves?

My friend travels to Rwanda with a camera
After the genocide to take pictures
Instead wanders grief-stricken for weeks through
Corpses–
Which is what we call dead relatives
Once they cross the line.

Returns with an infection in his heart
Which swells up grossly.
His semen dries up/
He pisses blood
Infected by the death all around him.
Doctors cannot name his disease,
But it's pretty clear to me what happened.

Another friend chains herself
To an old-growth redwood in Pacific forests
The logging company comes in anyways
Exercising eminent domain
With giant blades cuts the tree off above her head
With her strapped to it

We have perfected the Art of Death
While all around us eco-systems collapse
We kneel on necks

That are our own
We choke the breath out of...

In this neck of the woods, I remind
You the Empire is of War.

Did you not realize?

That all this time you thought
You were learning US history
You were being indoctrinated
Into the Art of War?

Did you not realize?

The model for all this
Sun Tzu clarified thousands and thousands
Of years ago

You learned to call it civilization but it is
Military strategy

To win a war
You attack not your enemy
But the strategy of your enemy
The psyche of your enemy
You sew division

Sound familiar?
A people united across difference

Inter-dependent as an eco-system
Less easily succumb to domination
Less easily permit the plutocrats of Rome
To plunder and decision-make
For them

Democracy my asshole
Never has this been anything close

Pursuit of Life, Liberty, and Property
For White Men

And then, begrudgingly for
White women

But MLK God bless him
And other clear-eyed radical brothers, Malcolm
Even Mr. Baldwin whose ambitions were more
Artistically focused than political per se

Those who saw with clarity
That indeed it was not simply the color of the balustrade
That gave the naming to the White House

Were impalatable to this goddam nation
That they built

Ergo Trump.

Ergo White Nationalism
Fascist revivals in Europe, etc.
Sons of soil losing their grip
On it
Gathering arms
Fomenting revolution
Would unhesitatingly overthrow the government they
Made because the premise of that government
Was never equality
That was pre-text to keep them in power

This was just the same way that Rome
Folded Jesus in, when it was convenient
Took the beautiful mystical teachings
And put them in service of Empire.

See how neatly that gets done?

The first part of the river, after flailing deep
Psychiatric medication
Lapses in hell
He'll never get better, they were told
My wife soldiering onward
Our daughter, three years old at the time.
Me deeply sedated on psychotropic medication
Returned home
Forty pounds heavier
As if the flesh were sandbags holding down my spirit

So it didn't go freaking off into the ether

My mind a tiny drip
Reduced from a massive torrent.
I remember about this time standing in front of
    the dishwasher unable
To comprehend how it functioned.

I could barely get dressed
Figure out anything.
Emotions flattened.
Mechanical rising.
So much medication morning and night

My brain burned.
Like a forest after wildfire.
Smouldering still.

It had been so much worse
Than even the worst I could possibly imagine.
But there I was

My beautiful beautiful daughter
Still needing me
Still wanting to be picked up
Still playing with my hair

My wife who didn't leave
God Bless You Lea Marie
Never has a man been blessed with truer

companion than thee.

Standing there in the bathroom mirror
My face ballooned a bit
I was thirty-seven
Looking at the pill bottles
Wondering was I about to take these
Or did I just?

The sound of my wife's heels in the hallway.
Talullah comes round the corner gleeful.

Oh my god.

Nothing about it was elegant, crossing the river.

For six / eight months it went on this way.
Making myself get up in the morning.
Making myself go swim.
What will I do all day?
My mind molasses no joke.
Couldn't read a word/ retain a sentence.

The forest burned to the ground.

I couldn't even mourn its loss anymore
Because I couldn't feel and
Because it didn't matter
And
I'd been in this new mind

So long now
It was just where I was.

The honey gone out of life
But still the life going on

At some point I go back to working.
How to explain where I have been to former clients?
I do not.

The fluency that before was effortless,
Now is barely there, but I have to work we need the money.

I take a job working with young men in prison.

Drive to Solano
A bleak penitential facility.
Sit with boys, nominally to introduce them to meditation.
Young men of color, mostly.
Who couldn't have given a possible shit
About any of this,
Mandated to a rehabilitative program.

I liked some of them though.
One who tells me I have woman's hands,
And at the time I can't help but agree.
A twelve year old white boy whose already had a

heart attack
From methamphetamine.

I sit in a prison office filling out paperwork.
It seems appropriate to the times in my own life.
I try to make sentences cohere
Explain what I'm doing with the youth,
Though I can barely keep the thread of a
    coherent conversation going,
Much less help someone else.

At a certain point I am asked to work with young
    men in the Oakland Unified School system
And giving myself a sober assessment
Realize that if I were them I'd not listen to a
    word this white boy said.

Decide I must engage in anti-racist training
If I am going to do such work

And sign up for a training with Lee Mun Wah.

It is 2013, apocalypse a year in my rearview.
I'm still marginally functional
Though now can load a dishwasher.

My daughter turns four.

I sign up for a workshop entitled *Unlearning Racism*.

I am in the car, driving to Berkeley, about at the
    intersection of 580
And the horserace track
When my body is seized by terror.

Some greater part of me convinced that I'm
    going to die.

Having passed through what I'd passed through
My initial reaction is, *You already did*.

But this grip of terror does not release my body.
My hands tighten on the wheel.
I consider turning around.
My body considers it greatly.
My breath ratchets up
I feel my heart tilting toward fight or flight.

I think of all the reasons that I have to suddenly
    cancel.
Call and tell them *I'm so sorry*
I cannot attend this workshop.

But I grip the wheel and do not turn around.
I drive into the fear
Like tacking a ship into the wind.

Closer I get to his house
Stronger the magnets in my body are pushed

away.

The training center in what my body perceives as ghetto.

I came through the gate with too much energy.
Sedated by medicine
Amped by my own fear

Knowing, in some part of myself that something is about to happen
Some medicine that feels like I am going to die, again.

It's why I say there was nothing elegant about this/
Crossing the river/
Abandoning our civilization

At no point did I gather beauty to my chest,
Speak gracious oratory
Paddle into sunsets

I went most of the way kicking and screaming
Pleading for another way
An exit
A release.

At this time I didn't even know there was another side to get to.

I perceived, simply, that I couldn't turn around

That the compact I'd made with the Divine/
Which I still couldn't feel
Was that in exchange for the husk of a body/
　　mind I'd been left with
My obligation was to pass through the fear

Have you ever sat in a circle
That seemed to connect invisible wires to latent
　　metals in your body?
Where other people's words hooked up magnets
　　to your innards?
Pulled on places inside you that you didn't know
　　existed?

This first circle with Mun Wah
Was like this

Perhaps the first circle not centering whiteness
　　I'd sat in knowing it was such.

My words when ushering from my mouth
Landed on others in ways I didn't intend
It was one long stumble
Foot in mouth
Embarrassment
Shame

False confidence and assertion

Nothing I'm saying is landing the way I mean it.
Maybe, says another participant, *you don't know
what you are saying.*

I tell you now, in hindsight, the next passage of
the river, the middle you might say
Was not me titrating off anti-psychotic
medication (though that happened)
But me titrating off of racism.

Gradually, over several years, I titrated off the
inner dose of racism
I had operationalized as an existential platform,
With Mun Wah, Rainbow, Peter, then D'Andre
all performing surgeries upon me at various
times.

It was, I am told, a long and complicated
procedure.
Most of the tumor was removed during a
yearlong procedure,
Though I suppose there is always the possibility
of relapse.

This was the second part of the river, I thrashed
across.

My heart, still during this time, and this is

> important to tell you
> Caused me to do things my mind didn't understand,
> But I had learned that if I didn't do them I would suddenly find myself in Hell.

> There has never in my life been a stronger motivator to listen to a part of me that I did not understand than this.

One time driving, after Mun Wah's training, I was headed home north on 580
When this knowing told my body - TURN AROUND.

Really?

Dusk was falling.
I take the next exit, already breathing easier, feeling like I escaped a guillotine, driving south now.
The highway unfurls for some time, 580 south, I realize I know not where I am heading.
At a certain moment I reach the exit for Coolidge Avenue, my body lurches toward it.
Ok, I take the exit.
Up, down, driving through the Fruitvale neighborhood–
And now a knowing is forming within me, I'm going to Peralta Hacienda Historical Park,

And my body begins to knot up.

In the middle of the Fruitvale there is a park
   so-called/
The Peralta Hacienda Historical Park
Home to the Peralta Hacienda, an 18th century
   house standing still/
And gardens.
I led a training there after my first unlearning
   racism training.

Took a break for lunch,
Heard, within five minutes, church bells and
   gunshots.
It is the bleeding edge of gentrification.
An ancient adobe/ community gardens/ swirling
   piles of trash.

Walking around the grounds, exhaling, well with
   the beauty of our circle
I encounter seven or eight young latino men
   lounging
Nod to them, one looks me up and down says
Be careful around here
& I, feeling at ease, thank him for letting me
   know.
Return to the classroom, sit down, feel a jangle
   in my body and realize,
Gabriel, that's not what he meant.
He wasn't saying, 'Hey white boy, just letting

you know there are folks around here who
might not have your best interests at heart.'
Indeed not.
It was a warning.

This is the place I find myself driving, dusk,
under compulsion, following directions.

Can you walk into that place humble enough?

Can you stuff off the carriage of your entitlement
that you drape over your shoulders in a lordly
way– and simply walk through someone else's
space without acting like you own it?

Can you peel off white body supremacy?

Now you find out.

I park, hands shaking as I pull up the emergency
brake.
Swallow hard, climb out of the car, lock the
doors.

It is a Tuesday night.

I walk into the park, praying.

There are latino families, children running
around.

Groups of teenagers.

In a fenced-in plot, a group of older Hmong
 women gathering some sort of bean.

Toward the back, a man seated beside a shopping
 cart staring into a grove of trees meditatively.

It is a village.

I, came prepared for war/ come prepared for
 death/
Afraid I will be killed

But it is only a village here.

The people are yellow, brown, black, red.

Not a single white person at all.

And I understand.
It is not that I was / am in any danger from
 them, really.
I am the danger.
I stand in the body of the danger.

I am the policeman / the US Army / the Bureau
 of Indian Affairs.
I am the Empire

The colonizer
The Great Destroyer.
This is who I have been trained to be.
My acculturation into whiteness.

I drive home, grateful in only the way you can be
    when what you thought was death turns out
    to be medicine.

Yet that night, I am seized by a deep terror.
A wave of fiery heat.
I feel the washing-over of a compulsion, and
    almost leave my bed near midnight to drive
    back to the Peralta.

At the threshold of waking and dream, I see, in
    the back part of the park, in a grove of tall
    trees strewn with trash, two structures that I
    had visited before without entering.
Two shacks, really.

When I walked near them in daylight, glancing
    in, they were filled with old mattresses,
Car batteries, broken crates, whiskey bottles

But here, on the edge of dream, I see stairways
    leading down into fire.
They are portals to hell.

There is, around them, some circle, some

ceremony going on, and the directive I am
receiving, sorting through, is to drive there,
and offer myself up as a sacrifice.

The thing within me that makes demands, when
it tells me to do something, is not to be
placated, reasoned with, subdued.

It pulls me out of bed, my hair stands on end.
Am I really to do this thing?

It echoes and redounds upon an earlier image I
had/
Before my mind had cleaved/
Perhaps a month into the 40 days of not sleeping
that preceded my private apocalypse
Where no longer able to control my mind
I considered driving to East Oakland and
offering myself up
Inviting someone to shoot me as a blood
sacrifice
Some way to atone for…

All this…

Harm.

Here, a year-and-a-half later, on the other side
of the abyss, my body shaking I wake up my
wife accidentally.

What's wrong? She says.

And I cannot explain it in any words in any way that would make any sense to anyone else.

She holds me.

I begin to weep.

I feel so guilty.
I feel guilt, in my body.
I feel complicity with all this error.
All this death upon the land.
What can I do/ how can I alleviate this reign of terror in which we are gripped.

And then, like the Angel of Death releasing me from its claws, the feeling falls away,
And I drop into dreamless sleep.

I could reel off for you, countless incidents like this.

Moments during this second stage, a period of years, where a knowing comes into my body, a certain feeling that I must follow, and suddenly something within me, unknown to my conscious mind, is navigating.

I visit neighborhoods, houses, knock on the doors of strangers, do all kinds of things I could never explain.

I learn to trust the compass of this feeling even when I don't understand it.

Learn to turn left, learn to set down the rock, learn all kinds of obedience to a force within or through me that I do not understand.

This is the second stage of river crossing.

It happens that, as well during this time, I titrate off my family of origin.

It happens that I find myself, sometime in 2014, two years after the apocalypse, after a minor bout of non sleeping- four days I think - I am titrating off the medication now, which has highly sedative properties, having a phone call with my biological parents, and without even seeing them, the sound of their voices makes the spirit in my body go crazy.

After talking to my mother I go lay down in my bedroom and it takes me a half-hour to retrieve my spirit from near the ceiling, where it has gone out of my body. Simply talking to that woman, the way she blows sunshine

up my ass, it sends me out of my body /
disconnects me from the earth.

Occasions that, in order to address all of this,
my brother and I engage a program of family
therapy with a woman therapist in Oakland,
sit all four of us together in a room.

My brother and I, in this process, hand back to
our parents all the parts of their own mess,
co-dependence/ warped boundaries that
rather than holding themselves they handed
over to us as children.

I didn't come here, into this incarnation, pass
into this river, through this apocalypse, to
carry my parent's luggage, to have them
leave it in my hands all this time. This we
tell them sometimes harshly, sometimes
gently, but basically make clear that we are
re-architecting our spiritual agreements with
them, and then do so.

This layer of interaction between us/
programming, is so deeply habitual that
only after four days of not sleeping, when
the ordinary mind's thinking is inoperative,
when the nervous system is raw, like the rocks
exposed along the bottom of a lakebed as the
water recedes, can I even see it clearly, but I

have seen it/ felt it/ named it in myself, and
I am not fooled by habitual patterns.

So disconcerting is this to my parents that they
make a story about me so convincing to
the therapist, a woman with thirty years of
training, that she becomes complicit with
them, breaks the clear boundaries of her own
ethical guidelines, meets with them privately
when she is under agreement not to, breaks
the boundary of the container that she has
established, I would say her name her just to
out her, that bitch.

This is why your mental health is shambles
people, your therapy weak in the knees. You
can't hold a boundary deeper than you've
gone in your own psyche, lady. If the roots
don't go down to bedrock, they will get
uprooted in a storm.

Psychotherapist removed, we meet as a group,
us four, continue the conversation until we
don't. My brother and I step back. My
mother leaves my father. He refuses to take
responsibility for his part in any of this.
Gradually, and then quickly I stop speaking to
him. There is nothing left to say.

We've excavated. We've gone all the way down

to the foundation.

I yelled at you, Father, yes, that's true. But you were young when you had me, and you were the only one who got to be angry my first twelve years. You were bigger and stronger and though not violent let it be known you would use force. So now you can man up, and take it when I dish it back.

I remember the moment when I became taller than you, I was sixteen, and from that time forward you made me sit when you wanted to discipline me.

It's not that I don't love you.

It's that the 'we' you keep talking about– the way you include me as if we shared a view, a perspective, as if I was standing next to you, looking out on the same world– maybe it existed when I was a small boy, but hasn't been true since I was grown, twenty five years ago.

A relationship is a living thing. You came to visit, took my car, went to the coffeeshop every day, didn't help around the house, did not once ask your granddaughter what she wanted to do.

I don't have time for the asymmetry relationship
   with you requires. I cannot stomach your
   self-absorption.

Change how you relate to me or we are done.

This I told you, clearly, gently, then very firmly.

This is the third passage of the river.
Again, not elegant at all.
I yelled too much.
Nearly punched him in the face.
I wish I had been calmer, but I was not.

Three quarters of the way across, thus.
I titrated off of racism, off of my family of origin,
   off of psycho-tropic medication.
All of that took six years.

7

ON THE SEVENTH DAY, REST

To celebrate my wife's 49th
We splurge and rent a modernist box in Sea
 Ranch
Drive north winding up the coast
Through Cypress, rock piles, sound of surf

Here it smells like saltwater, scrub grass,
 rosemary, sage
I sit at a table, before a wall of windows, looking
 out over the coast

Aging, I have to switch my glasses
One pair for typing and staring at the screen
Another to look out upon the seal rocks/
Watch surfspray, whitecaps
Cypress sculpted by consistent prevailing winds
 until
It hugs the shape of the hills

My thoughts turn to Perseus
On the north shore of Samothrace
Looking out likewise
Over the sea

The battle, in that case, is lost

Pydna behind him
He has retreated to the Temple of the Greater
    Gods
Seeking solace
Not protection
Awaiting the fate in store for him

The cinematic arcs of white capped
Waves rolling into shore
Cresting spinning cresting
He drinks in
All the beauty of this place
Inhales the morning
The warmth of the Sun
And for a moment forgets what he knows is
    coming

Twenty-two centuries later it is January 23
My wife last night shows me photographs of fires
    in Big Sur
Near a place we stayed two months prior
A coastline I know and love
An outlook where I stopped to photograph the
    lush beauty of the azure sea.

It is mid-winter, time of snow-capped everything
Many places
And there is a fire burning out of season
Across this land we know and love

I have survived wildfires now
Geographically, as it were,
The worst one though having happened in my
    mind
Some many years ago

In other chapters of this story I have told
Of a park in Oakland, the Peralta Hacienda,
Where one time,
Two years after that apocalypse, I wandered at
    dusk
Then came home, fell in and out of sleep
Awoke near midnight with visions
Of twin desolate shacks as the actual portals to
    Hell.

Some years after that occurrence,
Studying the history of Oakland
And the history of genocide in California
I discover something quite uncanny
That gives me great pause.

In 1822 the King of Spain,
Then Colonial Ruler of what was at the time Alta
    California
Deeds to the Peralta family a hacienda of 70
    square miles,
Ranging from what is now El Cerrito to San
    Leandro.

This deeding done,
The family settles in at first to an adobe
The first non-Indigenous dwelling in this part of California.

Unacknowledged in the history books
This deeded land is in fact unceded ancestral territory of the
Charchin and Ochenyo Ohlone people
Oakland, itself named due to the forests of the same type of tree
One foodstuff among many for these earth-based peoples

Their shell mounds/
Ceremonial sites are pervasive upon the land.
For at least two thousand five hundred years
They have been lovingly tending
These abundant forests/ marshes/ tidal flats
Ringing the bay.

The Peralta Hacienda,
Upon which this first adobe,
And then later a Victorian house was built
Turns out to be Ground Zero of Colonization
In my neck of the woods.

Turns out to be the epicenter from which,
Forthwith,
Issue genocidal orders

Turn out to be the twin towers of Empire
As it were,
The place from which genocide emanates.

In the state that I call home
Whose land I love
And where I feel at home

There were well over 300 massacres of native
    peoples
That remain undocumented/
Unmarked
Such that you can drive right past them no wiser
    whatsoever

Not a single plaque/
Headstone/ or
Marker/

No simple acknowledgement at all.

A list of these reads pornographic in its austerity,
    for example

August 1849, Raiders massacre 300 Wintu
    Indians, including women and children,
On the banks of the Moklumne River as they
    participate in a religious ceremony of some
    kind, no survivors, in retribution for the theft

of cattle some days previous.

Is a place not stamped with memory?

Does not what happens on this good green earth
    become registered in her?
The soil into which blood pours?
    The trees bearing witness to the screams, the
    groans, the crying of children?

My friend Tiokasin with Virgil Kills Straight and
    other Zen Peacemakers
Travel to Aushwitz in 2013 and conduct a
    Lakota ceremony there.

The rabbits puttering about, the deer grazing in
    the meadow still and prick up their ears
When he begins to call in the four directions in
    Lakota, listening

That place, Aushwitz, Birkenau, cannot help but
    carry the energies of death/
Of screams/ screaming / butchery.

A people carrying hell inside of them will create
    a hell on earth,
They cannot do otherwise I do not believe.

And so, my brothers and sisters,
I ask you,

Was it wrong then?
Strange then?
Crazy then?
That in my dream that night
After visiting the Hacienda, that I had no
 conscious knowing of
In my cognitive mind
Was the epi-center of genocide in my
 neighborhood…

Was it wrong then that it appeared to me in my
 dreams as the mouth of Hell?

Where do we get our knowledge?

    What is real?

    What do we believe?

    How do we come to know what we know?

These are questions of the ages.

Western civilization an accumulation, an
 accretion of knowledge inherited.

Passed down in causal chain/
The passion of the western mind

I took philosophy,

Understood somewhat the sequences of hand off
   from
Socrates to Plato/
Aristotle/
Various figures in the dark ages/ Beothius, St.
   Augustine worried about a pear
Leibniz
Newton, the Principia
Kant
Hume
Schopenhauer
Kierkeegard
Neitschze
Wittgenstein
Sartre
Derrida
Foucault
Those fucking Germans: Heidegger, etc.
Giants all…

Passing the baton of knowledge this
   accumulation
How are we to follow through all this map to
   find out where we are?

Gary Snyder, poet, comments:
95% of western philosophy is trying to figure out
   how to get out of the corner that we talked
   ourselves into.

But is this how we know anything?
Anything at all?

The toddler reaches out to touch a burning coal,
    glowing like a rose crimson jewel irresistible
Then jumps back stunned
Sucks back a long inbreathe and wails

She'll not do that again/
Try to pick up the fire like that

This is how we learn/
Direct experience

FUCK all this proxy shit we call education

What's required now is a great unlearning
Because

Rome fell.

Or hadn't you heard?

Something in me felt it.
Gazing down into the treetops/ those shacks
Not really filled with mattresses, dead batteries,
    bottle shards

But genocidal intent
Skeletons in closets

The blood of our Indigenous brothers and sisters
Fever dreams of conquest
Life, liberty, the pursuit of property

Terra Nullius
Grants it to us/
Another recruit for the Jesus of Rome/
Another coin for the coffers of the chuch

Education/
This apprenticeship of the mind/
Pulls us away from feeling

The knowing/
The tracking/
The dreaming/
The knowing of what came before/
In a pre-verbal language
A non-mathematical quantum mechanical
    language of intuition.

Of relationship.

How do we get free?
Perseus stares out upon the waters.
The Nike looks out from above.

This place,
And its religion, its ceremonies
Will twenty-two centuries later be known as a

    cthonic cult.
What does this mean?

Earth-based peoples/
Rites connected to the renewal of the earth/
The cycles of seasons.

We must tend to place.

He looks up at Nike, the statue,
And at the edge of dream sees her headless,
Blinks his eyes.

Sees her indoors–
What?
At a landing in a monumental staircase.

What is this?
    When is this?
Where is this?

Suddenly she is outside of time/
Protector of seafaring peoples/
In her proper place above the sea
Headless in a museum
Gawked at by people in strange garments/
Sudden flashbulbs exploding in her face
What are those?

Sees himself as a boy

Sees himself underground
The terror in him so thick it strips him from his
    body
Rips it from him as he has before
Stripped the skin from the carcass of a steer.
There is blood everywhere.

Heartbeat in the ears.

Twenty-two centuries forward now, it is I.
I am the same one
Who was there in Samothrace.
Same one there in Pydna.
Same one imprisoned in Alba Fucens.
    I remember it, I shit you not.

I repeated it again in this life,
Forty days without sleeping
My mind cleaved in two

Wondering what I had done to deserve such
Treatment
What harm I had caused that was so egregious/
but now I know it was a gift.

Had I been born again before this century
The psychiatric medications would not have been
    strong enough
To hold me down
And I would have lapsed off into madness yet

again.

Stripped out of a body like that/
That much terror/
Sewn into the spirit/
Takes a strong discipline to be able to accompany
Without leaving

    The Romans, when they captured me,
Paraded me through the streets of Rome
    manacled.
Put me in the dungeons where they held political
    prisoners.
Yet since I held ceremonial position
Had sought shelter in the Temple of the Greater
    Gods
Did not prefer to kill me directly,
Undesirious of incurring the wrath of Gods
They did not believe in
Yet nevertheless did not fully believe
Were unreal.

And so they kept me awake,
40 days,
In that dungeon
Having told me that they were going to feed me
To a monster
This thing with gnashing teeth

Having told me that they would make my death

Spectatorial

Like that scene in star wars where they feed Luke
To a dinosaur-like monster–
These are timeless themes–
And in the darkness
The sound of that thing screaming in my ears for
 forty
Days of no sleep

I lost gradually my reason
The mass of my body
All realm of reason
Until eventually slipped across the threshold into
 madness/
Death

It was lack of sleep the history books say that
 killed him.

But I came back
To try once again
Not at the birth of the Roman Empire
But at its death
Two millennia later, and here I am.

Did it again in this life,
40 days without sleep
I recommend this to no one/
Do not try it.

An empire is born
An empire dies

The center cannot hold
Mere anarchy is loosed upon the world.

I study all the western cannon
I can take
At Yale University
With other aspirants to the literary life

But that shape of that iron maiden
Is not for me.

I'd rather wander through the forest
My hand out before me ancestral radar
Tracking and sensing every living thing.

Convene a Council of equals.
Re-matriate the world.
Awaken the modern Indigenous.

I'd rather paint a painting.
Shape a stone…
Learn the Arts of Life
Not death.

So now you know my story,

Or a part of it
Ancient and
now.

REQUIEM FOR AN EMPIRE

I, who once was Perseus, Basileus of Macedon,
Hereby relinquish all pursuit of power/
All empires crumble eventually/

Dedicate myself forthwith
To guarding the circle of Life.

I am the great great grandson of the witches you
 could not burn.
I reclaim the moon as my mother.
The Earth, her daughter, is my home.

In this time of peril we have returned
To re-unite the tribes/
Lift up again the Old Songs
That never died
But have been sung by those subordinated
To the bleak vision
Of conquerors

No more
Will we stand aside
While land and mother are despoiled

We have returned to claim
Our Sovereign rights to Serve

What is Alive.

Begone from this place
All that is not holy.

Five hundred years ago
Cortez emerged from the belly of a ship
Enslaved the rightful King,
Mocetazuma,
In a place called Tenochtitlan
Placed on the throne a simpleton
And the world flipped over/
The ship belly up.

I tell you now the tide has turned
The boat comes righting itself

Stay close to the ground/
Be humble/
For the bottom becomes the top

    This great turmoil is the boat righting itself.
The boat is righting itself.
The boat is righting itself.

Know where you are.

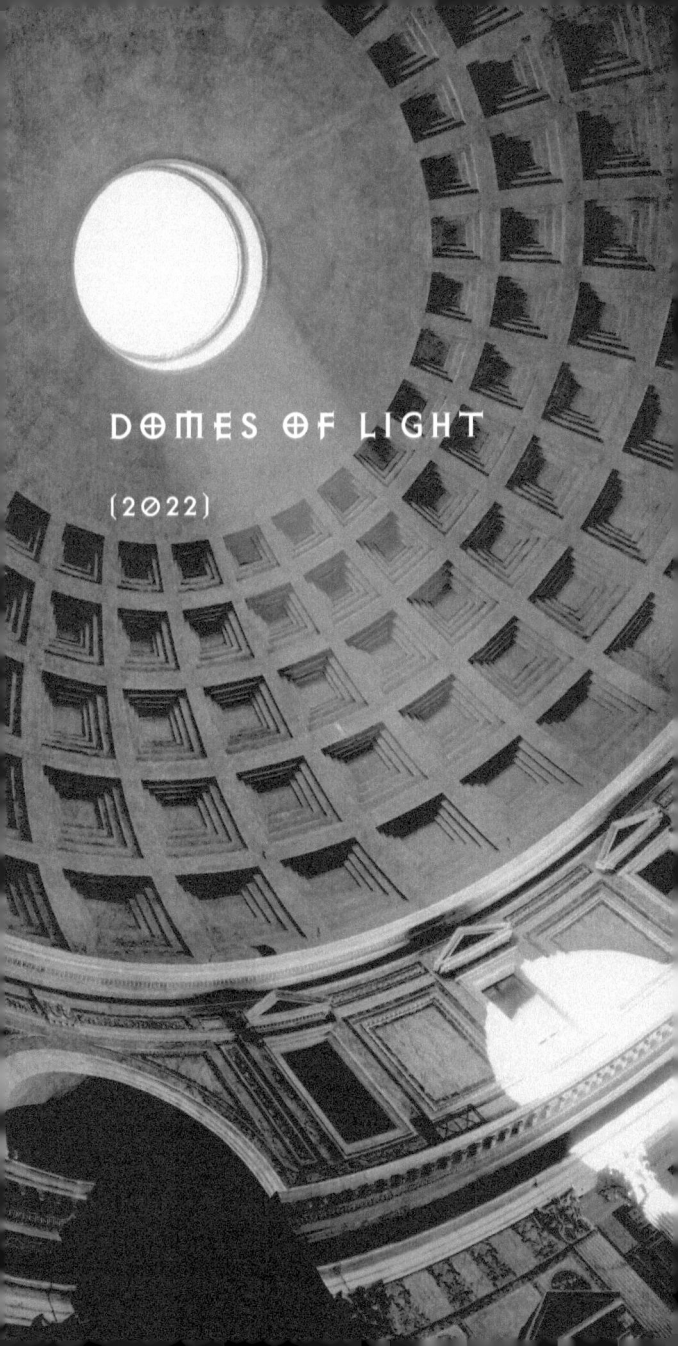

I

FOR PETE JACKSON, MARCH 16

These are dangerous days.

I didn't take a body, endure the pain of birth,
    pass through what I've had to pass through,
In order to hear stories about the Light from
    people who have heard stories about the
    Light.

At the grave of the Enlightened One I wept
    uncontrollably, couldn't stop.
Where are you? My heart aches to ask.
How could you leave us at a time like this?

These are dangerous days.

I have endured the collapse of my own mind,
    passed through it, re-built it, brick by brick.
The recreation of a slow temple, made of mud,
    hardened in the Sun, kiln-fired.
It took eight years.

Come to understand the grace in it all, that it
    was a form of Initiation.
What is made of brick, right formed, and set on
    the rock, that house the wolf could not blow
    down, we are thus taught as children.

Now the winds come, howling around us, and
    thatched roofs begin to fly, houses made of
    sticks fall all about us.
Promises made of thatch, economies made of
    sticks, corporations made of little more than
    paper.

Yeats says *Things fall apart; the centre cannot
    hold;*
Mere anarchy is loosed upon the world.

But we say things fell apart five hundred years
    ago.
The slow message has been making its way across
    the biosphere.
A telegram in dioxin, industrial poisons, greed,
    and extraction.

Since the moment the Original Instructions were
    over-written by the Doctrine of Discovery,
The moment Rome re-purposed the Humblest
    of Men, elided the Divine Mother from the
    teachings.

I say, *If it doesn't hold– it isn't the center.*
Root down now, into the center of the center of
    the center.

Carve out an inner reservoir

And put your ear to the ground there; listen

The Earth–she is alive.
Her heartbeat beckons and it is the heartbeat
 of your grandchildren's grandchildren as yet
 unborn
Looking to us to open a door to a world worthy
 of their becoming.

When, if not now? Who, if not us?

I didn't come for Enlightenment if it means
 anything other than holding on to all that is
 alive with all that is in my heart.

That's the only thing I'm doing here.

2

LOOK HOW AMAZING

Look How Amazing it is that We are Alive.

It doesn't have to be so.
Look all around us.

Entropy is the great law of the Universe, so we are told.
The second law of thermodynamics and all that.
The energy is supposed to leave.

But look at us.

Watch the two-year old toddling along giggling and hiccuping
Trying to put that butterfly in her mouth
And tell me with with a straight face the energy is leaving.

She's a tiny thermo-nuclear reactor wet-wired to a bleating
Beating heart and all around her energy is increasing.
It happens even if you look at her.
Eyes start laughing, hearts warm, smiles swim to the surface.

We know the village heart when we see it.

The force comes even into grandma's knees as she clings to them
You can see the old lady's whole body quivering with the transmission
And she is chuckling and clucking as she stirs the soup.

We are the evidence, you and I,
And the little ones tucked in at night.

We are the evidence that the physics of materiality only captured half
Of the picture–
And the bleaker half at that.

But it is important that we re-write the stories to account for this,
Because the limits of our stories are the limits of our imaginations.

And in a story of half-empty,
We author only half of our lives.

In a story of half-dead
We author only half of our possible beauty.

Consider that the credit markets do not want

you to be brilliant.
They do not want you to make dangerous
    courageous decisions/
To put your heart on the line.

They want you be a good little factory worker.
Spend coin on trinkets, re-model your bathroom
    again and again.
Do you need treasure sculpture and solid marble
    where you drop turds?

Has it occurred to you that your credit score was
    designed
To incentivize you to spend exactly as much as is
    most lucrative
To the banks?

As is most likely to keep your particular rat
Turning on the particular wheel
That your professional standing,
Status, income bracket,
And the Joneses down the street keep up?

To say the system is rigged
Doesn't do justice to how evil it actually is.

The Sun is a nuclear reactor
Pouring down benediction and Divine Light.

All you need to receive it is an open heart and a

solar panel.
A plant is a solar panel, don't you see?

A plant is a perfect solar collector.
Transforms sunlight into carbohydrate.
Makes oxygen.

Many of my business partners are trees.
We breathe together, feeding each other.
This is the Old Way.

Walk to work
And you are no longer financing Putin's army.

There are 5,000 gigatons of un-extracted hydrocarbons
Yet in our Great Mother
And all these drooling dictators of the world
Slobber to stick their fizzlestick dicks into her
    and suck out her lifejuice.

While Jeff, Elon, and Richard want to secret the
    hoard into outer space
And laugh at us.

We fund them, you idiot, with our radical failure
To renounce an antique worldview that says

There is not enough
We are not enough

Life is not enough

But look at how amazing it is that we are alive.

A honeybee dances in quantum code.
The Douglas fir's pollen comes down like a
    powder of moondust.

Our children look up at us for comfort.
In their tiny loins, the next unborn generations
    hold the question–

*Will you create a world beautiful enough to deserve
    us?*

Now is the time.

Wake up to the magnificence you really are.

3

LIFE IS BEAUTIFUL

From the smoking detritus of the cultures that
 died/
To the burning embers of those that yet live
Away from the stillborn perversion of that which
 pretends to be a culture, but never was
We must make a new fire.

We don't have to start it, because the Ancient
 Ones already did.
And those embers can reignite all of our hearts
 into flame.

What we have forgotten is what goes at the
 center of the village.
Skeena reminds us, for it is matrilineal.

If you want to create a village with a living heart,
 at its center goes the sacred fire. Everyone's
 duty is to (at)tend it.
What comes into the center of the village life is
 the child,
who is the hope for the future.
And holding the child is the Mother.

We know this image from many cultures.

In the west, it is the image of the infant Jesus in
the arms of mother Mary.
Yet this is an echo of older images.

In the gaze shared, by the infant and the mother,
we witness the polyvagally-informed mystery of
connection.

Ilarion reminds us that it is the dawning of the
Sixth Sun,
and in these days it is the duty of men to guard
the sacred work of women.

This sacred work of women, is the Mothering.
The Mothering is, of course, political.

Because the Mothering is the heart of the village
in action,
it is the remedy for the illness of the Age.

Those of us willing to take up the mantle of
masculinity, in a form that is not toxic,
have need to guard this Sacred work.
To us, the obligation to defend this Sacred heart
of Mothering
from extraction of all kinds.

A world that would like to gaze in, probe with
instruments, surgical and economic, and to
suck out the vital life force.

Is it any different than the way we stick our dick
 straws into the earth?
Sucking out the blood of plants that died in the
 carboniferous to power our lust for velocity?
Any different than the way Mark Zuckerberg
 sticks his algorithmic dick into the interstices
 of our inner lives?

For those of us who witness a great unraveling,
whose calling is to participate in a great turning,
the work then is clear.

It is not a gendered work.

One doesn't need to be a woman to participate
 in Mothering, or a man to guard the village
 heart.

One doesn't need to be a woman or a man at all.

One needs simply to understand that the word
 enlightenment,
as understood in the western tradition is a mis-
 translation,
as it is in fact the worship of a sky God, who is
 only half.

One needs simply to understand that half of
 Jesus' message
was truncated by the Roman empire for political

purposes.
That half, which was removed, spoke of the
   Earth Mother.

One needs, simply to understand, that an
   enearthenment is the other side.

The Hawaiians say it more clearly. In their
   language, the word *malama*
means to care for. Enlightenment then is
   malamalama.

To care for all that is.
Or better, to care for all that is alive.

This is the kind of tending required of us.

Let us find the necessary humility to learn from
   those who actually know how to do this.

Let us uplift the Ancient stories, the Ancient
   ways, the Indigenous voices, those who have
   been made small by the harms of multi-
   generational violence.
Let us put our technology at the feet of that, to
   serve.

Let us join hands in a great circle,
re-light the fire at the heart of the village,
and make our way home together.

Let us join hands in a great circle,
re-light the fire at the heart of the village,
and make our way home together.

Life is beautiful.

4

A PROPER ACCOUNTING

On the Seventh Day, in the morning, I have to teach.
So on the Sixth Day I set out to do a proper celestial accounting.

In one column, all the Things we have done to sustain Life
In the other column, what it has cost us.

Column One:

Took the Dragon's eye from my pocket and gave it to the 5-year old we encountered on the street on the day of her birth, so that she knew that the Universe is a mysterious place filled with things wanting to Bless her, because every child needs to know that

The other column: no Dragon's eye in the pocket, and so some need to replace that stone, which was my companion in times of need

On balance, I feel well with the transaction.

Blessing forward is blessing received, blessing the children is blessing life itself.

Column One:

Poured the full force of my heart into stewarding a forest, clearing deadwood, studying deeply the patterns of nature, carrying newts out of harm's way, not disturbing a swarm full of sleeping wasps, making covenant of non-interference with Oak known commonly as Poison, creating a small space at the edge of the meadow, building a cabin with my hands, finishing the walls with live-oak boards, laying the floor myself, cladding the walls, staining them ebony until my hands were dyed dark but non-toxic

The other column: thousands upon thousands of dollars in rent, ridicule from my wife (You rented a forest?), a year of weekends spent stooped over a wheelbarrow, various dust and sweat, a thousand hours of observation, a number of bouts of what is commonly called Poison Oak, every muscle aching, six months of carpentry, spending more money we don't seem to have, non-trivial splinters, hands dyed dark but non-toxic, no small scrubbing will remove

On balance, I feel well with the transaction.
Breath restored, work of the hands, thousands
   of non-human friends, a respite in the Living
   World, beauty so powerful it wounds, which
   is what is required to draw humans out of this
   trance

Column One:

Starting a business that is really a village, working
   80 hours a week for four years, refusing to
   allow it to be funded by a group of investors
   in Los Angeles wearing tennis whites, a
   group of investors in New York working for a
   Chinese Internet billionaire, a group of Angel
   Investors in Miami, various investors who
   talk about American football like I have a TV.
   Having to write the legal over from scratch
   because the law in America states that if I
   don't maximize profits I can be sued by the
   investors we did allow to join us.

The other column: My daughter was eight when
   this started, now she is twelve. Not so much
   left after 80 hours, in terms of time, in a
   given week. A million dollars spent, much
   of it that I didn't have, leveraged to the gills,
   a $180,000 loan against our home, credit
   cards maxed out again and again, stress to my
   lovely wife (you rented a forest at a time like

this?)

On balance, I feel well with the transaction,
  though it hurts, and I carry the wound.

A Lifeway recovered, a door to the ancestral
  future held open/
A new Old Way forward that moves in spirals
  and fractal arcs/
Placing technology in service to nature at the
  bountiful hearth.

The lesson of this lifetime, remembered from
  the last: Put everything you have into it; hold
  nothing back. These are dangerous times,
  give it your all.

Dearest celestial parents, I know you are
  listening: you can verify I have done so; you
  have visibility into all the accounts, seen and
  unseen.

Like most things in my life, I exert the moral
  right
To write the rules whereby my actions shall be
  judged in the Greater balance of the Living
  Law.

The Living Law which is the Living Word of the
  Living God spoken by Living prophets to

Living people, for this is how it is described
in the Essene Gospel of Peace.

And it is the Gospel of Peace that draws me in
a culture that preaches the gospel of War,
disguised as business as usual.

My accounts square up before the Divine.
As for earthly creditors, Jesus says give Ceasar his
due, and I will give him more than that.
But Rome wasn't destroyed in a day,
And I didn't come all the way back here, take
another body,
Wrap myself in a flesh garment again,
Endure the pain of Living to make things easy
for someone in a suit studying an actuarial
table.

I came to take back what is rightly ours: we, the
earth-based peoples.

The accounting that interests me is cosmological.
The economy we have been saddled with
destroys the only known biosphere in the
Universe as a daily matter of course.

Trust me: I will see it through to the other side.
I am trained by diamond cutters and I have come
to breach the fortress of arrogance.

At the tip of my spear is the most-focused cutting
   tool that exists: the laser light of love.

Stand aside, the Life Star is active, we are
   breaching Fort Knox as you read these words.

The Economy of Death has sprung a leak,
More are coming like us say the grandchildren of
   the witches you could not burn,
We are calling them home from across the
   Universe, back into play.

Hoard not your treasures here on earth where
   moth and rust corrode them,
But in the Spirit, where the celestial accounting
   takes place.

You have been put on notice.

5

THE DOME OF LIGHT

The diaphragms of the body are domes.
They are arches.

There is an arch between your heel, and the ball
  of the foot.
A dome in your knees.
A dome in your pelvis.
A dome in your respiratory diaphragm.
A dome in the roof of your mouth. (Why else
  would it be called a roof?)
A dome in the crown of your skull that had
  skylights when you first arrived; they are
  called fontanelles.

The first closes at 9 months, the second around
  18.
This is why, ancestrally, babies are swaddled for
  the first nine months,
Carried around on the back or the front of a
  caregiver,
bathed in the signal of the village heart.
Darcia calls this a womb with a view, though
  that's not her phrase.

We don't let the babies touch the ground until

the skylight in the roof of the roof of
The skull has closed: we want them carried
only by that which loves them, bathed in
the vibration of the Living Heart of the
Mothering.

We arrive here too soon; we are not finished
baking.
The dough is still rising when we enter the
world; not baked until toddling.
Not finished rising, really, until the pre-frontal
cortex is done- 25 years old?
(But never finished rising, really, for the
uninitiated.)
(It's not just your body that has to bake, but
your Belonging.)

Yet given these domes,
All these inward churches in the body,
All these spires and minarets designed to contain
the Holy,
We say - *Let the domes be filled with Light.*

It wasn't my idea.
It was a prayer received; spoken by a dear friend
in Stroud,
Handed down from Ancient Tongues, through
Ancient Ears to present hands.

Let us be surrounded by Light.

The Sufis explain this.

Light above, light below.
Light within.
Light in the heart
Light in the mind
Light in the skin.

Let your domes fill up with light.

I have stood in Rome, in the Pantheon, looking up, marveling.
That structure, over two thousand years old, is a perfect dome,
Monolithically symmetric, with an oculus at the top,
An open eye gazing at the sky.

I stood wondering aloud, to anyone who would listen–
How did they build this, two thousand years ago?
A marvel of engineering.

We are like this structure.
Domes of light; an eye in the uppermost for congress with the heavens.

After a ceremony, driving fast through green hills
    I wondered–

Can I open that oculus again?
Can I open the fontanelle spiritually? I don't
    want a mind that is closed:
I want a mind that is open

To Inspiration
To the dance
To the subtlest of the voices of the Gods.

I say, *Let your domes fill up with Light.*

The dome in the foot, let it fill up with Light.

What this implies, to me, there being a dome in
    the foot,
Is that your feet could know a thing or two
    about belonging.
Could know a thing or two about what direction
    to walk your body
To return to the Source.

In 2018, unable to decide in what direction to
    move,
Sitting with my friend Christopher outside, at
    the edge of Wildcat Canyon,
I learned to turn to my feet, the domes of my
    feet, the Light in my feet.

I let them have their knowing, which is not the
    knowing of the Mind.
And they steered me sure.

Can it be that each of the domes has its own
    knowing?
Our knees their own knowing?
Our pelvis its own knowing?

Making love from time to time, when the heart
    was open,
The moon was full, the wife was willing–

I've known this level of knowing from the pelvis.
It's dome of Light.

The breathing is its own knowing–
This for sure.
The breath a compass undoubtedly.

The roof of the mouth, its own knowing.

Each dome, filled with its proper Light.

There's a dome I'll never know wearing this
    man's body,
But my daughter is the good fruit of that dome
    filling.

Only women carry a dome of Light that large it
   seems.
Perhaps that is what frightens most men so.

Beings of Light birthed from domes of Light…

How come no one teaches us this stuff in school?

6

KALPA

Kalpa (noun- Sanskrit) The passing of time on a grand cosmological scale.

One cycle of galactic precession is accomplished
 every twenty-six thousand years
This celestial clock has just started over
We enter the Sixth Sun.

At edge conditions, phenomena accelerate bi-
 directionally.
Forces collide and intermingle, sometimes
 balance and give rise to third forces.
Quarks and sparks are ejected, imaginations catch
 fire
Riddles of the Ages resolve.

Lots of death and lots of birth.
My wife's grandmother has entered the stage of
 croaking breath
Haggard breath, labored breathing/
The death wheeze

Lots of Elders have been leaving recently,
 seemingly in waves
Big Brothers and Big Sisters,

As if moving to the farther shore and grasping
   hands to fortify us on the Other Side.

Bombs rain down in Ukraine.
The ordinary kind, and those called hypersonic
Moving five times faster than the speed of sound.

In my dream last night, unbidden, comes a
   dream of war.
I don't realize it is of war until late in the dream.
I am in the countryside somewhere, when from a
   distant hillside comes
A loudspeaker announcing something in a
   language I do not know.

And then, small from this distance– is it a couple
   of miles?
A projectile is launched, skates off into the
   distance at an oblique angle.

They've opened fire, I say.

The second projectile is launched at a different
   angle, an oblong disk,
A lozenge, it floats rather in our direction and I
   watch it, of a sudden,
Filled with something like vague wonder.

Half a click out it pauses, mid-air, like a Kite,
   these birds of prey that grace skies here,

Rotates twenty degrees, and continues, moving
    less obliquely now, more in our direction.

Still I watch. Five second pass, and now it is
    maybe six football fields distant, in the sky.
Pauses again, kite-like, rotates.

And like slow gears awakening in my body I
    realize it sees us.
Makes the final turn.
Incoming.

I remember having these dreams as a child,
Where you are trying to run away from
    something that is chasing you
But your legs don't work.

It is somewhat like this, labored, but I do not
    turn back.
I make myself run or force what passes for
    running.
There is an oak tree to my right, fifty feet ahead
    and I set my sites for that,
Thinking I can get it between myself and the
    blast.

I awaken laboring away from this projectile.
I never hear it land
Do not know if it ejects merely shrapnel
Or a dome of light.

The fifth Sun was entered,
Some say
When a proud God called *Tecuciztecatl* promised
    to throw himself into the Sacred fire
And hesitated, vain, fearful of his life.
In this moment, the poor and humble
    Nanahuatzin leapt into the flames and
    became the new sun.
Abashed by this upstart, *Tecuciztecatl* was
    shamed into jumping in himself, but the
    Gods knew two suns would overwhelm, and
    threw a rabbit across his face, so he became
    the moon.
It is why we see a rabbit across the face of the
    moon to this day.

This fifth sun was characterized by the daysign
    Ollin, which means movement.
It was prophesied to end with earthquakes
the people eaten by sky monsters.

Is a hypersonic missile a sky monster?
If we pray only to skygods, neglect their earthen
    counterparts, do we engender the sky
    monsters ourselves?

Can you understand what I am saying?

The older religions, the ones we would call now

chthonic, or earth-based, placed
One pole of the twin divinity in the earth.
Father Sky mates with Mother Earth, giving rise to all, say the Egyptians.
The prayer *Our Father* that Jesus spoke is only half of the benediction he gave.
Our *Mother which Art the Earth* has been elided from the scripture for political reasons.
Truly, there is symmetry.

As above, so below.
The mirrors of heaven and earth, reflecting one another.
Feminine and masculine in perfect union.
This is the way.

But peer back into deep time,
Observe the transition from hunter gatherer to agrarian society
Observe the accumulation of reserve
The dawn of accounting
The dawn of notions of accumulation, affluence, property, inheritance
Patriarchy.

From balance the scales tip in the direction of domination.
And the feminine is unwritten from the sacred texts.
Erased or omitted.

Why?

Is it not revealing that broad sociological studies
   tell us that if you give men extra money
   they will spend it on prostitutes, alcohol,
   fireworks, and religious festivals?
And that the women will spend it on education
   for the children, healthcare for the
   community?

Men want, it seems, more power, more pussy,
   more glory, more party.
Women want, it seems, Light in their children's
   eyes, strength in the village's bones.

I generalize, of course–not everyone is like this.
There are bitches and healed men too.

I think we men are afraid of the glory of women.

I think that we, wounded, are afraid of their
   wholeness, the monthly communion of
   blood,
The power of birth.

We've been trying to tame it since we were exiled
   from the Garden
Pointed at Eve and said to God- *She did it*.

That sounds like a story told by a man.
It was her, tempted by the Snake.

Have you noticed the way power ejects
  accountability from itself? Have you noticed
  the way whiteness projects sins onto the Black
  body?
How Black men become lazy, become rapists,
  etc etc.

Brother let me ask you–if you look in slaving
  logbooks, can you point out to me all the
  hours reserved in the day for the slaves to
  take siesta, fuck around, play at cards, get
  drunk, loiter?
No you cannot because there were none such
  hours.

Brother let me ask you–if you look sober at
  the law, can you explain to me how a slave
  woman, seen as property, brought into the
  master's house to serve…a beautiful woman,
  brown as a nut, seen as belonging to the
  master, was not raped?

Don't you see–we are/were the rapists and
  the lazy ones. The great art of storytelling
  propaganda was the displacement of this evil
  onto dark bodies. Our yearnings, inclinations
  interojected elsewhere: the perennial illusion.

Brokenness displaced.

And yet, this is always a kind of blindness.
A mental illness in fact.

Do you think it was any different with women?

Do you think Eve ate the apple?
Do you think she was made from Adam's rib?

Give me a damn break.

She gave birth to us.
We re-wrote the story.

Men with pens, drunk, in a room filled with
    prostitutes, at a religious festival, shooting off
    fireworks.
This ejaculatory fantasy passes for history, passes
    for mythology, passes for an origin story.

I come to clear the table,
To turn it over, like the money-lenders table in
    my Father's House.

I am here to clear away all that bullshit.
We do not have time, anymore, for such
    children's story.

Clear the desk of those ruinous rough drafts,
Burn that shit
Smoke it in the fire and watch above, there rises
    a Dome of Light.

Yesterday I left the religion of which I had been
    part for fifteen years.
And I felt profound relief.
It came in waves, slowly, washing over the shores
    of my body.

I pursue relations with the Source directly.
Unmediated by a priest, unmediated by someone
    else at all.
Unconfused by what someone else has heard
    about the Light.
I know the Light in my bones.
I know the earth she is made from.
I know the sky she rises into.
I know the Moon and the Sun.
I know who I belong to.

Twenty-six thousand years, this cycle, and
    observed from a certain distance, a certain
    remove, we begin to see the arc, the
    trajectory.

Old cultures knew that worlds end and begin.

Balance obtains, and then the scales tip.

Domination unfurls, like a fern opening, widens
   its grip.

And then a *kalpa*, vast celestial time unfolds,
   narratives resolve back into their beginnings.

For the dying the world ends everyday.
For those being born it begins.

Choose to be born.

When the eye is single the whole body will be
   filled with Light.

Choose to be born.

7

MURMURS

A murmuration
Endlessly reforming itself
Above fields of winter wheat.

The way dewdrops pull down a single thread of
    spider silk bending
beads of light into caternary arches inverted.

A conversation
So deep it has no bottom
Registering all the way down
Like a rock falling endlessly
Down a well with no bottom

Applying mystery to all things.

How did we become convinced that Heaven
Was only up?

What literalists, we.
Prayers only to the Skygod, as if He
(Masculine, is it not?)
Were sole doorkeeper to the miraculous.

But why do we want, so dearly,

To transcend?

To go up?
Why not go down?

How did down become equated
With the low?

Water runs down.
It finds the lowest point.
Its humility is its service.

Is water not high?
Is water not a manifestation of the light?
Does the light not do this– serve all?

How did down become equated
With Hell?

What about the good earth?

Says Solomon in the psalms–
The Lord is my shepherd I shall not want
He maketh me to lie down in green pastures:
he leadeth me beside the still waters.

Beside the still waters.
This is low.
Settle your body upon the blanket of the earth.

What literalists, we.
To believe that the Light.
With capital L is gone at night.

What about our Grandmother, the moon?
Our ancestors, the stars?

What of all this?
What of the inky dark
The velvet dark
That is filled with mystery
wonder &
Silence.

Is this not also of the Light?

How did we get so confused?
To equate white with purity
And black with evil?
Cain and Able.
Afraid of snakes.

Literalists, we.
Afraid of that whose belly hugs the earth.

No–
It's a lie.

It's the echo of an earlier lie
Fashioned into propaganda,

the power of words misunderstood
An error in translation.

Literalists, we.

The womb is dark.
Is the womb evil?

She is where all of us come from.
Are our mothers evil?

When you close your eyes is there no light?
What of the inner light, then?

We are hamstrung by language.
The straight path speaks not of gender.
These are unfortunate collisions
Between bigotry and linguistics.

But it's easier, is it not, to judge?

To make a hierarchy in our minds
Good/bad
Pure/impure
To draw up a framework…
One true church.

Do you know how many have told me straight-faced
That their religion is the one true path?

That their lineage, granted by revelation,
Is THE WAY.

It is said that Jesus
Instructed
Pray to me
but
Do you speak Aramaic?

Because he never said anything
Of the kind.
Not a single word in English ever left his mouth.

A game of telephone
Rome serving as operator
A mis-translation of the Aramaic
Into Greek
Into Latin, a dead language
Into English.

Pray as I pray were the words.

In the manner of my humility
My devotion
My faith

None come to the father but through me we are told.
Impossible he would have said this.

What is the motive, friends?

If someone has a lock on your salvation–
If they've convinced you heaven can't be had
    here on earth–

Does it not serve the purpose of those who
    conquer
Who would plunder you of your Sovereignty
Of your joy
For you to believe only in an afterlife

To treat this life
As though it didn't matter?

Only a people afraid of Life, I say to you
Seek transcendence.

Why not rather be here?
With us?
In a circle?

Why not permit the glory
To pass through the flesh?

Do you think it an accident that you have a
    body?

Do you think you were made in the image of the
    Divine

So you could kneel down and wish you were
somewhere else?

These are the fever dreams of a traumatized
civilization
A people stranded homeless
Evicted from the Garden
A people in exile.

Come home.
Come home to the perfectly imperfect.
The particularly human.

The illness that is this civilization
Claims salvation
For those in Exile.

But the path back from Exile
Isn't necessarily religious.

It could be, but it isn't necessarily.

It could be in finding enough safety to grieve.
It could be in finding enough humility to admit
we don't know.
It could be in finding enough silence to simply
listen.
It could be in finding enough trust to share.
It could be in finding enough courage to be
touched.

All of these things bring us down to earth.
They bring us down into our bodies.
Into contact with the ground,
Who is a She.

Her dome of Light is terrestrial.
The mind's eye opens like a needle pushed into
The cushion of the heart.

Through grief
Brokenness
Surrender
There is a way.

It is not talked about so much.

Not glamorous, perhaps, in the way of
    transcendence–

Toad Medicine, Heroic dosing, psilocybin, et
    cetera et cetera

Have you ever cleared debris from a creekbed
Choked with deadwood
And felt it thank you?

The dome of light could be underfoot.
Pearlescent eggs under a rotting log that you
    leave undisturbed.

The stone polished by your care.
The softness of pine needles.

It doesn't have to be grand, the awakening.
Not only big bangs and all-nighters.

It could be doing the dishes,
Scratching the dog's ears,
Scooping the last bit of ice cream out of the tub,
Mending the shirtsleeve.
The needle silver under halogens
Darting back and forth.

It could be that simple
If you were really here.

The key to unlock
Is the doorway to the heart.

It is written–
When the eye is single, the whole body will be
    full of Light.

8

SPATIAL GEOMETRIES OF THE HUMAN FORM

From molten core/
Seed and stone
Bone.

From soil
Muscle.

Mycorrhizal networks
Nervous system.

Salt waters
Blood

Carpet of grasses
Skin

From Vortexes
Sacred sites
Portals
Acupuncture points

Songlines
Meridians

They say we are made in the image

Ten fingers
Ten toes
Eyes to behold
Singled
Then filled with Light

A beating heart
At the Center
Leba

The pith
The marrow
The center
The best part of anything

Yet Earth they say
Also, in her various layers
Condensed
Long ago

And it appears
We are made in her image
As well

Hermes Trismegestus says
As above, so below.
As within, so without.

Is it not so?

Yet if we are made in the image
And the image is of Her
Is she not herself

Divine?

Truncated from the scriptures/
Elided/ silenced
Split in half/
The teachings.

Our Father, which Art in Heaven
Our Mother, which Art the Earth

So said He also
Because it is so

Earth creatures, we.
Of her,
Of our Mother.

I clamor thus into the forest
Peer down into the deepest stillest pool
To see how it is inside myself

Gaze vividly upon each stone
Study their opacity, heft, geometry, properties
To know what I am made of

Whisper to the fungal network
To understand how I am ensheathed within

The study of Nature
Knows not a boundary between
Within and without.
It is One.

How then, have we gotten
So estranged from Source?

Ineffable verb of
Sacred mystery
Gift me the experience of union.

Heal my separation
Transforming it into an embodiment
Of Belonging.

DOMES OF LIGHT

Is it ok to be deeply well at a time like this?
It seems, somehow, an insult to the very
    zeitgeist.

For what is demanded–
Not even asked–
Is that we be crazy with worry
Or denial
Our heads buried in the sand
Or running around like chickens
The severed parts
Whose heads are not buried.

What if–
No!

What if
fuck all that
in the gentlest possible way…

What if
What is required
Is deeply sober wellbeing?

What if what is required

Is Sovereignty

Dedication to equanimity?

Unwavering focus
On what serves?

What if we become unavailable
To what distracts us?

Unwilling to indulge
What harms us?

Fiercely focused
On what we are fighting for–

Which is Life.

Clear your schedule.

Comb through the list of contacts on your phone and cull it.

Go through your list of excuses,

Write them down,
Then burn them in a ceremonial fire.
 Confront yourself.

Stand naked before the mirror

Of what you came here for–

And ask–

What is the necessary work?

What is to be done?

Aware, in all likelihood
That much of it is an un-doing.
And more yet a non-doing.

It is the emptiness of the pot that
Allows it to carry.

Make space
To be filled.

You are a dome
Meant to carry light.
That is your proper and necessary work.

How can you do your duty
When the still space inside you
Is yet unborn?

Even in the emergency
Find
The center of the center of the center

For only from that place
That womb
Is birthed the Knowing

Of your particular
Why.

Of what particular
Light you are meant
to shoulder

Create the conditions
To ignore
The emergency around you

And attend to the emergency of
Your own Soul

Which knows

This is the moment.

APPRENTICE TO GRIEF

(2022)

APPRENTICE TO GRIEF

Grief calls me, first softly.
Then a drumbeat so loud I feel my heart is on
 fire
And yet mistake her for rage.

When I was much younger
Seven years of age
The grief held me under water
'Til I drowned.

Took a crucifixion of sorts
A rescuscitation
To bring me out of that,
37 years in the making.

This time it's different.
The grief comes as fire,
As immolation
Not drowning.

I burn in grief.
I mistake it for rage–
But No, parts of it *are* rage–
But grief.

This time, she accumulates slow and I do not
 notice.
Until four, five, six events and my heart is on fire.

Passing through this cannot be done alone, I am
   told.

Did you know that the Empire forbade
   mourning?
Which empire?
Most of them.

That energy too powerful to be spent
On people bent to the drumbeat of
Recovering their sovereignty.

And so mourning was outlawed.

Look at how far we've come.
We've come nowhere.

Now the interdiction has been internalized.
We suppress the mourning in ourselves.
The Empire has no more need of doing it.
This is called internalized oppression.

We used to weep and gnash our
Teeth
Tear out our hair, beat our chests bloody.
But now we (the collective we, of whom I speak)
Drown in it, sink underwater
Into depression
Into diseases of despair,
Not even bothering to reach out to one another.

This will not get us anywhere except dead.

So what is the other way?
What is the way of reaching out in grief?

I am not familiar with this technology.

This form has not be taught me in this un-
    culture
Into which
I have been socialized.

And so I come today, with others,
To apprentice to grief.

Let grief be the teacher,
Not some facilitator,
But grief herself.

Grief–
Teach me to bear sorrow as a living wound
Teach me to wash it clean in the waters of
    reverence
Teach me to transmute it alchemically in the fires
Of prayer and valediction
To sing your song of which my heart has much
    need
And which has not been taught in my mother
    tongue,

Birthed from Empires of loss.

Can you do all that, please?

Let us venture forth and inward, we shall see.

⊕ ⊕ ⊕

It is November 12, after the second rain.

I have mulched the better part of the new garden.

What griefs do I carry these days, I wonder?

Of those known,
the leaving of a spiritual path,
Some turmoil in a marriage,
The daily wounds of difficulty,
Financial struggle and the rest,
Loss of intimacy under stress,
A falling away by choice from my family of origin.
Trials and tribulations of work,
The great difficulty it has been.
Betrayals from institutions I was told represented
The pinnacle of success.
People structured in systems of domination
And exploitation hovering round and seeking to extract.

The loss of a dear place, this one, as pen meets paper,
Strikes as fire in my chest,
And perhaps deeper yet the unknowing of what to do
About this rape of the land
Legal according to the letter of the law,
A rape in my comprehension of the Living Law.
And beneath or behind all of these the *wetiko*,
The cannibalizing force,
My chest is hot to name it,
Our civilization so-called itself.

These are those griefs carried close enough to the surface that I know them,
Held in the bubble of what I consider to be my individual sense of self,
And yet intuitively I sense these are fractal apparitions and intimations
Also of grievous collective losses.

Spiritual.
Companioning.
Familial.
Financial.
Institutional.
Capitalist.
Bio-spheric.
Civilizational.

Sing in me muse, and through the forked byways
Of your tongue
Let this polysyllabic rhyme be sung.

I bring objects for the altar of grief.
Some to burn ritually,
Some to place.

In the former category
My old uniform of spirituality,
Which I intend to alchemize in fire.

In the later *the Odyssey* of Homer.
Imprint of the western cannon.
Archetype of the hero's journey,
Nostos, the longing for home
At the heart of this failed project
Of western civilization killing us all.

⊕ ⊕ ⊕

Dearly beloved,
Please forgive me the short notice.
I am traveling to Lagunitas
For a grief ceremony that my spirit
Calls me to.
It is required somehow to enable me to step
Into the moment that comes next
Carrying less weight.
Phone if needed.

Love you,
G.

⊕ ⊕ ⊕

What am I grieving?

The sudden village.

The lack of a permanent village.

Exile (self-imposed) from the village I thought I was a part of.

Come in fact to burn the uniform of my prior spirituality,
To alchemize back to its original soil
My Indigenous spirituality
That took up the mantle of a particular religion,
A particular walk,
A particular formation of ceremony, cosmology.

Yet not only that.
I am grieving the over-take and over-reach of whiteness.
I am grieving rape & pillage of land.
A family of origin I have no wish to talk to—
No wish to remain in dialogue with.
Betrayals by institutions
I have been trained to look up to but not only

that.

I am grieving perhaps my socialization
To toxic desires,
Into conformity with deathways,
Into believing in progress,
Into believing time exists.

It changes everything to know I will
Read this aloud,
And so I am grieving sloppy ritual–
And yet, whatever–
I am grieving the rules,
The chastening bell.

⊕   ⊕   ⊕

My original beauty got so deformed
By the shitstorm of the irrelevant place where I
    grew up.
Fuck St. Louis.
Fuck Olivette, Ladue, Clayton.
Fuck the midwest bourgeois suburban flightless
    boring shitbirds of my youth.
Fuck the close-minded bigoted traumatized
    incestuous victimizing socialization
Into whiteness of my family of origin.
The atheism of the monster philanderer patriarch
    perched above my youth.

Fuck my family of origin,
Their petty misbehaviors,
The monstrosity of my grandfather
The passive vacuum of my grandmother's
    evacuated self

Fuck my peace-maker mother
My personality disordered father
Fuck the smallness of mentality
Fuck the smallness of those shitty suburban
    strident lives.
Fuck all of that.

Do I sound angry?

You stole away the beauty of my childhood–
for what?

For some notion of family a fantasy never really
    there.

You moved back there, fearful, fell under the
    mantle of protection
Of the grandfather, a monster,
A judgmental patriarch, failed and falling inward,
Philanderer,
Playboy,
Out of control in your boundary violation.
Fuck you.

Fuck my parents in their weakness,
Their smallness,
Their victimization
Their inability to read social cues, class.
Their inability to keep us safe.
Fuck you.

Fuck you to the smallness of mind that is St. Louis.

Fuck you.

Do I sound angry?

I grieve the time I wasted there.
I grieve the ugliness of that place.
I grieve waking up in the second story room of my youth,
Pallid light.
Imprisoned by that place,
And the suffocation that being there was.

Let it be.
But fuck you first.

Perhaps all this will change after the doorways of compassion open.

But first–*NO*.
Fuck you all.

⊕ ⊕ ⊕

Escape velocity at age 18.
Roped back in at age 19.
Escape again at 23 for good.

I look back now, from here,
Hands planted in earth,
Trees all around me,
Down a dirt road in the mind that is the recovery
Of my childhood beauty
At the mess of that madness.

What a loss.

Outside the window here there are towering Douglas fir trees.
The light is good and strong even in November.
Fuck you, I spit that history out of my mouth,
The residue of a time I could not find myself.

Here there are palm trees and the variegated thrush of the mind.

What is this grief?

Am I good?

Has the storm passed?

The sky is blue enough.

Rage passing through and then…

The silence in its aftermath.

No bones broken or plates shattered,

Just words poured out on a page

In the quiet of the mind.

Here we are in a grief ritual.

The morning is passed, we have come together in circle.

Into the technology of another culture that knew how to contend with loss.

I grieve.
I grieve.
I grieve.

The simple act of allowing it to exist, all we have suffered.

Exists anyway, whether we allow it or not.
But–ah, just this, just allowing it.

The body understands even if the mind does not.
This rest,
This repose.
This relenting of the contraction of defense.

A descent.

Dante knew something of this, did he not.

Nel mezzo del camin de nostra vita
me ritrovai em uma selva obscura
che la diritta via era smarrita.

But I am not lost.

Breathe down into all this tightness,
The lamplight heart
The heaviness of it all.
The burn of fire.

I sit with my back against the hearth,
The right side of my face warmed by flame.
Outside a stellar's jay calls,

The wind is chilly but we're alright in here.

We all are alright in here.
⊕ ⊕ ⊕

What am I alchemizing?

Religious clothes that don't fit anymore…

But then it takes me awhile.

I wander, until, *YES*

Being pinioned by struggle.

Heartrate picks up, that is closer to some truth.

Some small spherical hard stone.

Fake rocks.

Poverty.

That tightening fear.

I am alchemizing poverty.

And the mindset of poverty.

Of not enough.

Of sometime in the future.

Of not yet.

Of not now.

Fuck all of that.

I am alchemizing getting screwed.

Fuck Stanford, fuck all of that.

I am re-writing the mystery code of my own becoming.

I am grieving religions that do not fit,
That cause one to give up parts of one's sovereignty.
Of struggling, and letting that be in the rearview.
Of poverty, of not enough, of not being there yet.
This is enough, this moment, here, now.
Of getting screwed.
I am alchemizing getting screwed.
The inter-generational trauma of getting screwed.
Because of being Jewish, or being traumatized, of having lost one's parents, or being afraid, or whatever else stands in the way of sovereignty.

I call on the mystery to transmute–
I don't know how–
These griefs into whatever is through them.
Whatever learning needs to come through them.
Whatever needs to be set down, left here, on this
    land, which is not my own.

Whatever needs to be burned to ash.
Burned to phoenix.
Burned to dematerialize.

Part of a uniform.
A stray autumn leaf.
A fake rock.
A mushroom.
A screw.

Strange alchemy of fire.
Mysterious guardian of becoming,
In my chest already, work your becoming
On my bundle.

Let's have a ceremony.
Soon
soon.

⊕ ⊕ ⊕

Ah, grief.
Your gift is the deeper arc of my own yearning to

be free.
Is the shape of the shake of the rattle.
The sound of the drum.
The remembrance of the body's ability to shake off what is not needed.
Beneath the hollow of the hollowed out chest,
In the hollow of the collar bone
The deep seat of the sits bones,
The gift of grief is the shape of life–
That suffering the deep counterpart of love.
Love lost.
Love suffocated.
Love turned in on itself,
Given no place to turn.
I will set you free, if I can.
I will give you back to the altar,
Set you before the ancestors,
In a sacred way,
Not disclaiming you,
But letting go the suffering of your stagnation.

Grant you a place of honor,
If I can,
Acknowlege your knowing,
For here I am,
In this ritual from another people,
Another tribe
That my body somehow knows how to do.
And for this I am grateful,
Though grieving,

For these five doors of grief.
The grief of transience, all things changing,
Of the seasons, of time, of age, impermanences.
The grief of love not touched.
The parts inside me where love had not entered,
Forgiveness had not worked its way in.
The grief of ancestry.
This one I'm still working with,
Whose ancestors are mine,
Ancestors of spirit or blood,
I question yet.

The grief of mystery.
The grief of the world.
The grief of existence.
Counterpoint to love.
I can see how rage is the stepping stone before
    your door.

I don't know what has happened in this ritual.
And perhaps that is part of its intelligence.
Yet whole, I feel somehow,
Through the tears falling steady as autumn rain.

DESCENT

We moderns are not good at descent.

Grief is a descent.

We want to go upward
outward
worship skygods.

Build rocketships
and colonize Mars.

Grief has a downward motion.
It hollows us out.
Makes our spines bow
until the belly becomes a bowl,
so we can gather
there
beneath
where we customarily
identify as self.

Grief anchors us
to the viscera.

We want thoughts
and prayers that rise
ethereally

to the celestial

But grief–
her intuitions come
with our nose pressed
to a crack in the earth

from which some
deeper older exhalation,
Pythian perhaps,
exudes.

Grief,
like all elemental
motions,
all attributes of love,
is hosted by the body.

Our body wears
her,
could be adorned
by the earth-based
knowings
she gifts us,
deepening through
our footpads back
into soil
and the knowing we
are home
in the animal, vegetal, and mineral realms.

Grief could
give us beautiful
gestures of mourning.
Abilities to allow
tears to flow through.
Make us like rivers.
To our people.

Grief could make us like fire.
Burned to the ground,
immolated by her immensity.
She could make us
into pheonixes,
if we let her.

Grief could be a purification.
A kind of moisturizer
for the spirit,
if we rubbed her
on our bodies
with reverence.

Alternatively,
denied,
for those who
refuse to acknowledge
the collapse wing of creation

Grief could,

exiled,
adorn us with madness.
Adorn us with suicide,
adorn us with matricide,
adorn us with homicide.

This might look like
the proliferation of opiates
and firearms.
This might look like
knees on necks.
This might look like
the Amazon rainforest burning.

This might look like some
of today's authoritarian
leaders.

What if there was a camera
that could photograph their exiled grief?

Instead of merely Putin,
Trump, Bolsonaro, Xinping,
we saw their ghostly
disembodied grief doppelgangers?

Cooperative societies
welcome the stranger,
but, we,
the moderns,

were birthed with the formalized
exile of the Other.

We take all the darker,
wilder parts of ourselves
and place them outside
the circle of our self-knowing.

You know what I'm talking about—
we are storytelling creatures all,
the colonial enterprise wasn't merely political,
but a psychic colonization.

Enslaving the dark bodies,
subduing the Indigenous bodies,
was the subduing of the wild unknown in
    ourselves.

Was the banishment and sterilization
of the sovereign in each of us.

And yet, these ejected parts,
still they twin us,
unknown,
the invisible gravitational forces
twisting our yearnings into deathwishes,
for beings split off from
their deeper intuitions
cannot but hasten death.

We call it dark matter
in physics
(these inexplicable twins).
What are they made of?

Exiled grief.

If we confessed that as a culture,
our current motions of response
to pain—
numbness on one hand (opiates)
fighting on the other (firearms)
were inadequate to the purpose of mending our
　　hearts,
what would we do?

We would humbly apprentice to grief.
We would ask for her assistance to make us
　　whole.

To do this, we would have to let her back into
　　the house.

And as she took our hands in her own,
we would find ourselves descending,
and we would need to allow this.

We would need a community to do this with.

And we would need to unstory our thinking that

we know where she is taking us,
for as foreign as it feels,
it is in the direction of home.

DESTORYER
OF
EMPIRE
(2022)

I DON'T NEED A LICENSE

I don't need a license to break your heart.
I don't need a diploma to dance on your bones.
I don't need to pass some kind of test to speak
    truth to power.
I don't need your stamps of approval.

For some reason I cannot fathom this same tiny
    kinglet
Alights on Queen Anne's lace beside me
When I am grieving
And greets me with a single eye so sweet and full
    of light
It is like a blackberry about to burst

For some reason I cannot fathom
No matter that I don't deserve it
The good earth holds me up
Even when my mind has collapsed

Gives me food to eat
Air to breathe
Provides me shelter

And an intricate beauty
Makes me weep when I dwell overlong upon it

From the crash of waves,

To being truly seen–
It makes me shiver,
These moments of being alive.

This body I am wearing–
I did nothing to earn it,
Yet here it is

Capable of feeling depths of sorrow,
Breadths of tenderness
Aching solitude
And complete accompaniment.

Of soaring and burrowing,
Of feeling everything
Or shutting down completely.

And through this body the greatly
Strange music of becoming plays.

How entirely unexpected to have a body at all.

Again, nothing I did to deserve it.

⊕ ⊕ ⊕

I don't need a license to help you mend your heart.

We don't need permission from your doctor or

your therapist.

We don't need to ask to re-ignite the sacred spark
of vitality.

Or to learn to practice restoration.

But it will take a village.

We don't need permission to help heal the world,
but it begins with ourselves.

Each and every one of us.

Imagine the original fireplace,
The hearth around which the village gathers.

Keeps us warm at night,
This place where we come storying together.

Where music and laughter well up,
As the flames lick the night awake.

Where children are tended,
Elders listened to.

A place where we have time enough for story,
For reverence,
Where we set down the cares of day,
Pick up our handwork.

Around the circle, at night,
Is literalized the truth
That those sitting farthest across the fire
Are the ones who see with most clarity what is behind me
Invisible to myself.

The word Jesus spoke,
That has been transliterated as Sacred
Was *Qadash*, in the Aramaic.

Qd- the centerpoint
Ash- the circle of light and heat radiating around it.

The fireplace is at the center.

There is no head or tail in a circle.
There is no hierarchy.

Get right with it.

We come teaching three things, which are one thing.

1) Healing
2) Sovereignty
3) What it takes to inherit our possible beauty

Put things in order before they exist.

This is the way of the beings of the ancestral future now.

We are calling you home.

THE VASSALS OF ROME

The vassals of Rome have come
20 plus centuries after Pydna
to lay their heads in my lap
pleading
heal us please.

Have come to the
Destoryer of Empire
trusting,
doe-eyed almost,
believers
in the miraculous
powers of
our work
about which they have been told.

Their heads are here
I watch the heartbeats pulse
through carotid arteries
my hands under their necks
remember the caryatids
doomed to hard labor
for siding against the Empire

I hold the heads
of the vassals of empire
in my hands

These heads
where the stories of self
have been located,
who have come to be healed.

Whose hearts are ill–
do they know, really,
this sickness they carry
the mind virus
of the *wetiko*?

Come meek
as do these
vassals of the cannibalizing
force.

Curious
and intellectual,
volunteering
to receive the cure.

I watch the blood
pulsing in their necks.

Is it vengeance
I contemplate still?

I remember
what you did to my people.

I know who you are.

Your progenitors
cut the heads off our gods–
toppled them into the ocean

Me you killed
in the cruelest possible
reverential way,
cowardly.

It was a bad way to go.

And now, you are here
asking for my help,
pleading
heal us.

And I can see that you
are suffering,
through from the look of it,
the disease you
have is not what has been
commonly diagnosed.

It's a blood disease,
really,
will require
theragnosis,

an atonement.

Possibly a blood
sacrifice.

That was what you made of me.

Twenty centuries of enslavement.
This is the crown I wear.

The mark I carry,
in the twelfth house.

You have come to me,
the enslaved sovereign,
you servants of the crown,
asking for my help,
asking to be delivered of your suffering.

What shall we do?

How will I destory you?
So much hinges on the placement
of two small letters.
An *r* and an *o*.

Ro or...
De - stroy or story.

My hands have been instructed to heal.

But none other than Socrates said
Practice to die.

What I bring you now
will feel like death.
I will almost kill you.
It will be very close.

I will squeeze you within
one mortal inch of your life,
and watch the blood drain from your face
in the recognition.

I will hold your life in my hands
As you have held hostage all of life

You have come to the neurosurgeon
surely you realized,
lying down upon my table,
that I could take your life
in my hands

The knife is out
I weild it dexterously
never a finer swordsman
will you come across

I shave within a hair's breadth of your life.
This nerve,
it is the fineness of a human hair

and this close then
hangs your life.

By a thread, they say.

Consider what you are asking of me

You who killed my people

You who murdered my lifeway

Destroyed my culture

And those of earth-based people
around this sphere

Consider what you are asking of me

To spare your life?

And why should I

You came of your own volition
set your head in my lap
innocently enough

but do you understand who I am?

And more importantly–
do you understand who you are?

20 centuries of deathfuckery
ye white people

ye people devoid of color
devoid of culture

ye blight upon the land.

there will be blood

it wells up
from the neck
from the wound

you grow light-headed
here in my lap
swoon
enter a sort of fugue state
dreamlike

an assembly
of images loosed down
the lacelines of the nerves.

You who dwell in palaces.

You who deal in human flesh

recoiling from images of yourself

selling other people
setting fire to villages
laying waste to crops
murdering infants

you scream out
cower in a corner

in the dining room
the cold stone floor is relentless
the dining table
is heaped with piles of carcass
in the center of the table
served on a platter
with an apple in her mouth
a human woman

Knives out
at the ready
all of you standing in a circle
the chef's knives at the ready
she is still alive
as the flesh is flayed
and you eat

you are crying
now
but this is the truth of it

this is who you are
who you have become

you are cannibals
all.

I hold your head in my lap
there is blood everywhere
your blood
my blood

but I will not pass out

I have trained for this
endured the descent
passed through the gates of
hell already several times.

Heironymous Bosch has nothing on you
look at these wildfires
the scorched creatures
the apocalypse unleashed by Rome.

And for what?

Jeweled rings on fingers?
The luxury of strawberries in winter?

Our only home desecrated
so you can binge-watch Netflix

and doomscroll on your iPhone.

The vassals of Rome have come

The vassals of Rome have come
20 plus centuries after Pydna
to lay their heads in my lap
pleading
heal us please.

Heal us from
anxiety
depression
hopelessness

Heal us from
social media
the New York Times
Xi Jinping

Heal us from
the mounting casualties
stock market volatility
the profit and the loss

And you are bleeding out.

Did I make that incision?
Or simply peel the bandage off
that old wound?

I'm not completely sure.

I study it now.
This thing that has been asked of me.
By you,
but also by All That Is.

You've come, resting your head
here
not for a bloodbath,
neither a suicide or a homicide

but as if to say,
genuinely,
help us.
It didn't turn out how we thought it would.

This is not the story we came to tell.

We thought it was a hero's journey–
it's turning into mass suicide.

But I am the great destoryer of empire.

The hero's journey,
that is part of the problem,
its particular origin.

Because the hero's status depends on elevation.

And elevation immediately implies
its opposite,
generating the schizophrenia of supremacy.

And it is this dualism
generates all that follows.

The impulse to heirarchy
at the root of the root of Rome.

To be above
implies its opposite.

What came before you,
the motherist's way,
was not hierarchical but flat.

Was not an -archy at all,
but a circle.
This is the old new way.

You aren't a hero.
Neither are you the devil.

You are no more
no less
than any of us here,
our feet standing upon this earth,
dependent upon her for everything,
helpless as a newborn babe,

whose mother provides every nourishment.

How did we forget our proper place?
And more importantly, how do we resume it?

The Empire–
its entire history
origin story
existence:
a deviation.

That is what I came to say.
A deviation of dominance.

All you have been told,
a lie.

This story of survival of the fittest
this Cartesian
and Darwinian
myth is
but that.

We have come to destory
empire.

I am the great destoryer of empire.

Not me, but the nature
moving through me

My vengeance
thus,
a new narrative identity

I gift you second sight
a blood mirror

I will not shirk
my duty
of showing you who you are

Will not spare you

will not flinch

out of courtesy
and determination.

I've waited over two thousand years
to be here with you

Came back to be enfleshed
again

I know who I am

I remember what you did to me laſt time.

My mercy is in part

my steadiness

This hand holds the blade steady-
it doesn't flinch,
doesn't shake.

At some point,
as you lie there
beneath the knife,
you'll have to choose whether or not you trust
    me.

What will well up in you is to call me a murderer,
to believe I am coming for your life.

And I will not try to dissuade you.

Flinch one micrometer, and indeed you will be
    dead.
It will not be my hand or the knife that moves,
But you shivering against it
That will be enough to sever that nerve.

And that nerve is all that binds you to this life.

I did not come to play.

But steady yourself there,
at the flaying edge of my scalpel–

Steady yourself where I cut along
the nerve-bed

Where I trace your lifeline
Cutting away what is dead

And you'll find something different.

I know the cadence of the Lifeway
The rhythm of burial and resurrection.
Winter in the body and the coming spring

it flows through the marrow of my bones

We can gate you across the threshold

into a new old world

An ancestral future worth remembering
An ancestral future worth inheriting

Just don't flinch.

Your head entire
And all carried within it
is in my hands.

Your proper residence is the heart.

My job:

Help you find your way back there.

Just don't flinch.

DAWN ON THE LAST DAY OF THE FIRST DAY

It is dawn on the last day of the first day.
Hawk calls.

Yesterday's tomorrow beckons.
A patricide in the dreamworld.

Rain,
which we sorely need,
but the day dawns dark.

At 5 am, sitting in my studio,
I am pulled from contemplation by a whine
of metal
through the rain

I assume some county officer
has come early to unscrew the lid from drains–
assume that outside it is flooding–
the water pooling–
this how immediately my mind makes story,
how seamless.

I walk outside to discover
a startled neighbor
her Prius jacked up in one corner
dishevelled and breathless in the rain.

They tried to steal my catalytic converter
for the 3rd time, she tells me.

Brazen attempts
before sun-up.

Desperate days.
Those objects filled with metals,
they are melted down,
an insatiable alchemy
values them in the black market

dreams of sustainable transport
derided.

It is the dawn of the last day of the first day.

Today, I believe, fortune will smile.
In the hubbub of the haste of obligation
I've nearly forgotten what brings me joy

So hard I've been pushing
this shoulder against the unyeilding
mass of Empire for so long

And today, there is some final resistance giving
    way

I can hear the snapping of bones

the breaking of locks
turning in their tumblers

We are ready to step out of the dark tunnel
of our becoming into what is next

Many years ago
I wrote

the red vortex of cowboy
death licks its chops
in the kiosk of my halogens

this fragment
loosed from a future self
arriving to me at twenty-three,
twenty-four years ago now,
sitting there in a grim apartment
in St.Louis unable to see
my future

I was smoking at some indeterminate
hour of the night.

I look back now,
the future self foretold
the one who would inherit
those twenty syllables
marvel at them for years–

what does it mean?

before placing them,
like a stone,
into the matrix of this poem
with finality.

Who are we &
why are we here?

Do you know
who you are?

Do you know
why you are here?

I came back.

We are all coming back, all the time,
in all ways.

To finish something
started many lifetimes ago.

To bring the chord progression
to resolve.

It's the accident of an
expressive eyebrow
make dogs man's best friend

And I haven't been able to
afford to go see a dentist

Four and half years of 80 hours a week,
and this year I've lost 250K I didn't have

but it's an illusion–
time–
I have been grinding this edge
for lifetimes

repaying a blood debt.

the failure to give it everything
upon everything–
in truth, I held something back

And this is the price I paid

It can be beauty
and grief
and rage
all at the same time,
this I know.

Civilization:
Is it a fight or a gathering?

This is the question.

History a gathering that turned into a fight.
A village that went to war.

Stranger welcomed
to stranger exiled.

This is the nightmare of history.
We have forgotten who we are.
We have forgotten where we come from.

In the lust for the spoils of war–
land, treasure, women, slaves:
we inadvertently sold our own souls.

There comes a reckoning,
a clarification
an apocalypse:
truth revealed.

But the turning of the table,
the righting of these millenium-spanning
wrongs,
it is a fight too,
don't kid yourself.

History
a village turned into a war.

The ancestral future
turning war back into a village.

It's a fight
don't kid yourself.

A fight to put ourselves back together.
A fight to find common cause.
A fight for the power of love
over the love of power.

I didn't come to destroy
empire,
but to destory him.

And empire is not a woman.
Not a she,
not a mother.

Empire is the father,
the patriarchy
the worship of skygods
for sure.

You don't kill the father
you re-write the story

victors narrate the history.
but the herstory?

Who tells that?

At the heart of the narrative
there is always conflict I am told

But at the heart of character
yearning

What then if the yearning
is for the village?

In the middle of writing these lines
I am interrupted
by someone trying to sell me an unsecured loan

the phone rings incessantly these days

So many snares available to us

⊕   ⊕   ⊕

And everything seems so much harder than it
    needs to be

Was it really necessary
To return
Two thousand one hundred years later
take a body

Pass through all of this anguish

all of this effort

Just to remind you
remind me

that the human heart
doesn't live inside us
but between us?

that human happiness
isn't inside
but together

that we are a village

needful of a hearth at the center
needful of all the children
elders & musicians
storytellers all

of mothers and fathers
sisters and brothers
strangers on arrival
people different than us
whom we don't know

that what appears as Other
are the unknown parts of myself exiled–
come back so I can extend them hospitality

That we need everyone–
the dogs,
the stars,
the dogstars,

the morning thrush
that strange insect the children are afraid of
even the village idiot
from time to time

That there is no me
anyway

Nothing solid
here

all on loan from
a benificent universe

clothed in the apparatus
of a flesh garment

There's the goddam phone again
uncanny almost
distraction on demand

Look what a fabulous
edifice of civilization we have built.

We can be distracted all the time.

⊕ ⊕ ⊕

Was it really necessary
to build all of this grand edifice

of technology

just to realize it will never call us home?

There's a bifurcation
happening

A speciation event

One line will
continue to worship
skygods
build phallic altars to the Above
we will call
spacecraft

And leave behind this
celestial orb,
our Mother.
They might succeed
in uploading their consciousness
into a computer
succeed in becoming
avatars in a metaverse

escape the agony
of starvation
deep adaption
fires
and the blood and shit
and devastation
down here

Yet as certain as day
follows night
and night follows day
that is the language of Empire
endgaming itself

And like a brief candle,
one day...
out out

I've been trying to tell you there is another way.
It's much simpler,
but that doesn't mean it is easier.

It is the way of the ancestral future.
The way of the circle.
The way of turning back towards the pain.

The way of the village.
The way of the collapse wing of creation.
The way of grief, as appropriate response.

The way of hands in the soil.
The way of cooperation.
The way of the small band hunter gatherer.
The way of moonlight.
The way of lullabies.
The way of 99% of human evolutionary history.

We sing the collective awake.

The way...home.

Unstory the empire
in your own private mind.
Unstory the empire
in your public life.
Unstory the empire,
come back down here
where feet touch the earth
where our heavenly father
meets our earthly mother

set the damn device down

Come back to where the inbreath
is twinned with outbreath,
rise with fall,
the cadence of heartbeats,
breathing,
the sacred unity
alaha ruha.

home.

I have crossed the river
descended

bringing back news
to my people.

The village is within reach.
Make your way carefully
across the rocks,
do not slip
do not be distracted.

Just on the other side of this ridge

It is where I am coming from

Set down all your excess baggage

Steel yourself for the passage

It will take everything in
you not to look
back

Not to glance at the screen

But don't

There is no more time

It's now or never

Echoes of Rome fall away

The sound of a phone bleeting into the void

Someone somewhere wants to sell you some insurance

Rise up sovereign self

Son of the Sun
Daughter of the Moon
Child of Earth

Inherit your possible beauty

Fulfill the prophecies.

Become who you were meant to be.

Become a real human being.

Become an ancestor.

Become
Become.

Be.
Come.

In order to complete this–
whatever *this* is–

I have had to break, at one time or another,
    every rule I was ever taught,

Oh the Grief!

except one:
to thine own Nature be true.

Te ao marama

Hold fast to the center of the center of the
    center
while everything collapses
and trust.

This is the way–
surrender &
reclaim your seat
at the table of Life.

Natureza Gabriel *is a connection phenomenologist and neural cartographer.* He is Founder of Hearth Science, Convener of the Restorative Practices Alliance, and Co-Founder of the Academy of Applied Social Medicine. He is Host and Executive Producer of The Restorative Practices Film Series, *and the* Connection Masterclass. *He is the principal architect of the Restorative Practices Neurodevelopmental model. He is the author of* Restorative Practices of Wellbeing, Keywords: A Field Guide to the Missing Words, *and* How Whiteness Operates. *He lives with his family on Miwok territory in South Salmon Nation. You can generally find him in the forest, gathering words, or building a giant hearth.*

https://restorativepractices.com

www.ingramcontent.com/pod-product-compliance
Lightning Source LLC
Chambersburg PA
CBHW030549080526
44585CB00012B/320